ADVANCE PRAISE

"This deeply intelligent book is full of scientifically grounded, practical help for a wiser, happier life. Succinct, heartfelt, and soulful. Highly recommended."

—RICK HANSON, PHD, AUTHOR OF *HARDWIRING HAPPINESS: THE NEW BRAIN SCIENCE OF CONTENTMENT, CALM, AND CONFIDENCE*

"A physician offers sensible reflections on finding the path to a life well lived."

—ADAM GRANT, *NEW YORK TIMES* BESTSELLING AUTHOR OF *ORIGINALS* AND *GIVE AND TAKE*

"Sanj Katyal masterfully weaves philosophy and psychology, timeless wisdom and modern research, deep analysis and practical tools. This book can help you fulfill your potential for success and happiness."

—TAL BEN-SHAHAR, BESTSELLING AUTHOR OF *HAPPIER* AND *CHOOSE THE LIFE YOU WANT*

"*Drawing from eastern religion, modern psychology, and ancient philosophy, Dr. Sanj Katyal has transformed himself and, in the process, has given us Positive Philosophy: Ancient and Modern Wisdom to Create a Flourishing Life. It is the book he says he wishes he could have read twenty years ago. Readers of this book can profit from the insights he has gained in those decades.*"

—WILLIAM IRVINE, PROFESSOR OF PHILOSOPHY
AND BESTSELLING AUTHOR OF *A GUIDE TO THE
GOOD LIFE: THE ANCIENT ART OF STOIC JOY*

"*If you want to live a good and meaningful life, read this book. From philosophy to psychology, you'll understand what great thinkers advised for living well and how to put that advice into positive action for a better today.*"

—MEGAN MCDONOUGH, CEO, WHOLEBEING
INSTITUTE AND AUTHOR OF *A MINUTE FOR
ME: LEARNING TO SAVOR SIXTY SECONDS*

"*Sanj Katyal has written a wonderful book—wise, well researched, practical, and inspiring. He offers the rigorous findings of psychological research as seen through the lens of timeless wisdom. The result is both beautiful to read and useful on a daily basis as he helps his readers to use the best of science and philosophy to make our lives happier and more meaningful.*"

—LYNDA WALLACE, AUTHOR OF *A SHORT COURSE IN
HAPPINESS: PRACTICAL STEPS FOR A HAPPIER LIFE*

"This handy little book is full of wonderful wisdom-based treasures acquired from ancient philosophy and positive psychology that you can begin to use immediately. Dr. Katyal weaves a sensitive, thought-provoking story by using the tenets of philosophy and psychology, and by courageously exposing his own vulnerabilities to help us connect with what most of us struggle with: fully realizing our own potential. He details a simple-but-not-easy path to living a flourishing and meaningful life."

—JOHN BEITER, PHD, EXECUTIVE
COACH AND PSYCHOLOGIST

"This book is an excellent, concise blend of insights into well-being from religious, philosophical, and scientific sources."

—LEE J. MARKOWITZ, PHD, ASSISTANT PROFESSOR
OF PSYCHOLOGY AT LA ROCHE COLLEGE

Positive Philosophy

Positive Philosophy

Ancient and Modern Wisdom to Create a Flourishing Life

Sanj Katyal, M.D.

LIONCREST
PUBLISHING

POSITIVE PHILOSOPHY
Ancient and Modern Wisdom to Create a Flourishing Life

ISBN   978-1-61961-485-7 *Paperback*
        978-1-61961-486-4 *Ebook*

This book is dedicated to my family.

Contents

INTRODUCTION

It is possible to live well, even if it must be in a palace.

—MARCUS AURELIUS

The book you're holding in your hands is the one I wish I'd read twenty years ago.

Starting out as a young man, I thought the Good Life was built from a secure job, plenty of money, nice cars, and a big house. I followed the blueprint our society lays out for its youth and traveled down the path of traditional success, earning professional degrees and building a standout career in medicine. I have no regrets about my decision to become a physician; I've been blessed. What I do regret, though, was the cultivation of an "I'll be happy when" mentality that carried me through my younger years.

I'll be happy when I make the dean's list. I'll be happy when I get into medical school. I'll be happy to be done with training and making more money. I'll be happy when I'm married. I'll be happy when I have kids. And so on.

Somewhere along the way, I realized that this never-ending cycle of pursuit and achievement did not lead to fulfillment. Life was good, but I wasn't living the Good Life. While I felt grateful for all that I had, and the opportunities that had been given to me, I had a growing sense of a deep unrealized potential in myself and my family. The potential to do more, to make more of an impact, to feel more, to love more. The potential to live an extraordinary life.

Unlocking this potential has become my life's work. I want to live a more authentic, joyful, and meaningful life. I want to stop sleepwalking through life and fully experience each moment. I want to stop getting what I want and start wanting what I have. I want to stop accumulating and start giving. I want to stop living by society's default value system of enlightened hedonism and start living a principled life of integrity, gratitude, and service.

I've gathered everything I've learned and put it into this book. It's meant as a tool for anyone looking to flourish. This book offers a set of rules that will help you be more present, form better relationships with your spouse and children, experience more tranquility and less stress, become a better person, and ultimately look back one day on a life well lived.

To be honest, I'm writing this book for my kids. I want to provide a concise framework for the timeless truths and modern research that I have found to be most useful in the path toward a flourishing life. I also feel a sense of duty to share these truths with anyone who may be trying to find fulfillment themselves.

What I hope most of all is that my kids can use it as a guidebook for their own happiness.

THE CULT OF BUSY

Whenever I ask someone how they're doing, the answer I most commonly receive is "busy, really busy." We've become efficient in the use of our time, but are we effective? Many people are suffering from stress, anxiety, poor physical health, and general discontent. They have spent their lives getting to a perceived destination, only to feel empty and unfulfilled upon arrival. The working philosophy of most of these people is one of enlightened hedonism, interspersed among periods of the work required to fund their pleasure. They live and work for their weekends, vacations, and retirement; they're subconsciously, and sometimes overtly, obsessed with the pursuit of pleasure and the avoidance of pain. I know this cycle well—I was one of those people.

As I began to look around me, I knew there had to be more to life than simply avoiding as much pain and pursuing as much pleasure as possible. What I was searching for was a deeper level of well-being than the transient emotional state that many describe as happiness. I wanted to flourish. The problem was, I didn't exactly know how.

What does any lifelong student do, when confronted with a search for knowledge? Hit the books.

THE OLD MEETS THE NEW

There is a common theme that runs throughout the ancient wisdom of philosophy: the recognition of unrealized potential within all of us. This potential may be envisioned as dharma, duty, true self, or inner light. Human potential is a force that takes on many names, but no matter what word is used to describe it, the concept is the same across cultures and histories.

Aristotle said that the ultimate goal for a human is to achieve a good life, a state of eudaimonia, or flourishing. He and other philosophers advised that the path to the Good Life is to realize one's full potential through the use of reason, contemplation, virtue, and service. One of the reasons this ancient philosophy still resonates today is that it illustrates an ageless human condition: we all want to flourish and live lives of meaning. We want to raise good kids who will be better off than we are. We want to have fun. We want to be fully present and deeply experience each moment.

The goal of philosophy is to teach us how to live well—how to make sense of our place in the world, to better understand suffering, to discover which goals to pursue and how to pursue them, and to realize the best way to interact with others so that we may one day look back on a life well lived. In short, philosophy teaches us how to flourish. Ultimately, we flourish when we fully realize our unique potential in life and use this potential in the service of a cause larger than ourselves.

While the goals of philosophy are noble and right, the paths to achieve those goals are often not clear. What can we do each day to ensure that we stay on the path to flourishing?

This is where the modern tactical tools of positive psychology can help. Positive psychology, often called the science of happiness, offers evidence-based strategies to improve well-being. It focuses on human flourishing rather than alleviating distress.

My introduction to positive psychology was through a

book called *Happier*. I love this book. It provides a model of happiness and strategies for becoming happier that are rooted in science rather than metaphysics or pop psychology. The book's author, Tal Ben-Shahar, has gone on to write many more books, but perhaps his greatest claim to fame is that he taught the most popular course in Harvard history: Positive Psychology, with over 1,400 students. I reached out to Tal and asked him how I could learn more about the concepts he introduced in his book, and he invited me to apply for a one-year intensive certification in positive psychology that he was running.

It was during this course that I met Tal and heard him lecture in person. What was most impressive to me was his ability to "bridge the divide between the ivory tower and Main Street," as he often stated. He effectively translated evidence-based research findings into a format that was entertaining and easily understood by anyone. Meeting Tal in person was a pivotal moment in my life. He was engaging, present, and accessible to all of us. In him, I saw someone with an analytical nature and deep respect for science that was using his abilities to their fullest potential, and essentially devoting his entire life to helping people live better.

I shared with him my idea of this book—a book on how to live better that I wish I had read twenty years ago. Not only was he supportive, he offered to read the draft! Tal has gone on to start several companies that focus on spreading happiness on a much larger scale. He is indeed living the Good Life, and I'm always thankful that he took the time to respond to my initial email. His response changed my life.

POSITIVE PHILOSOPHY

As I deepened my study of philosophy and positive psychology, I realized that both had their limitations and advantages. Philosophy holds a wealth of guidance, but its ideas and concepts can be challenging to integrate into daily practice. What exactly does living a life of virtue mean and how can one live this way? How do I find my dharma, or sacred duty? What steps should I take to fully realize my unique potential?

Positive psychology offers more of a functional blueprint, but many people have incorrectly focused on happiness as a transient emotional state rather than the original focus on human flourishing. Platitudes and quick-fix slogans have arisen over the years—"Happiness is a choice!"—that discredit much of the more substantial, evidence-based findings of the field. Even the word "happiness" is so overused that many don't really understand what it means to be happy or to come up with a plan to become happier.

In order to develop a roadmap to flourishing, I combined

the best of both fields into what I call *Positive Philosophy*. It's a daily code of living—time-tested principles that are based in the ancient wisdom of philosophy and validated by modern evidence-based research. It returns philosophy to a set of practical rules of living well, rules that are backed by science rather than opinion. Positive Philosophy preaches a focus on character development over material accumulation, tranquility over popularity, appreciation over expectation, presence over productivity, potential over possessions, and living the Good Life over having a good life. It allows us to proactively act on what is within our control—our thoughts, goals, and actions, instead of reacting to what is outside of our control—others' opinions and behaviors, life circumstances, and an ever-changing universe. We need Positive Philosophy as a personal operating system for an optimal life, one that consists of a fully realized unique potential in the service of the world around us: a life of flourishing.

THE BOOK I WISH I'D READ TWENTY YEARS AGO

This book outlines a personal operating system, Positive Philosophy, that allows human beings to flourish. In this book, we will explore the ancient wisdom and philosophical teachings of Aristotle, the Bhagavad Gita, and the Stoics. This will allow us to understand the critical relationship between concepts of eudaimonia (flourishing) and dharma/sacred duty (fully realized potential).

We'll also examine the relatively new field of positive psychology and discuss modern, evidence-based strategies proven to increase well-being. We will explore key concepts such as hedonic adaptation, mindset, mindfulness, essentialism, and grit as tactical tools to unlock our full potential. We'll conclude with a daily action plan designed to implement the above strategies immediately. This plan focuses on simplicity and effectiveness to create a personal operating system that has been proven to move us closer to our eudaimonia. With it, you'll have the tools you need to start living the life of virtue, service, and tranquility you've craved.

PART I

THE PAST

CHAPTER 1

LESSONS IN HAPPINESS

I want to be happier but don't know where to begin. What does happiness even mean?

What exactly does a good life look like? If I ask you if you want to be happy, the answer is "Of course." If I then ask you what it means to be happy, the answer becomes less obvious. The problem with the word "happy" is that it denotes an emotional state that's often regarded as transitory. "Yesterday I was happy, but today I'm sad," or, "I will be happy this weekend when I don't have to work." This type of happiness is not what Aristotle was referring to when he stated, "Happiness is the meaning and the purpose of life, the whole aim and end of human existence." The word that he and other Greek philosophers used was eudaimonia. Etymologically, it consists of the words *eu* (good) and *daimon* (spirit). Eudaimonia has been loosely translated as "happiness," but Aristotle and other philosophers, including Seneca and Marcus Aurelius, thought of eudaimonia more as human flourishing, or optimal living, rather than as a transitory emotional state. This flourishing life can be viewed as a model for others and as a life well lived.

If we shift our focus from trying to be happy to attempting to live a good life, we can use ancient wisdom from religious and philosophical texts, along with modern, evidence-based research, to craft a road map toward this state of eudaimonia. It's important to understand that, as Aristotle searched for the highest good in life, he explored many popular concepts as potential candidates. The pursuit of pleasure was often seen by many, both during and following Aristotle's time, as the highest ideal. Certainly, hedonistic pursuits of modern times follow this tenet of pleasure as the main goal of life. But Aristotle readily dismissed this concept because both cattle and humans can pursue and experience pleasure. Therefore, because pleasure is not unique to humans and can be achieved by base animals, it cannot be the highest goal of human existence. The next concept he considered was honor. This also was quickly discarded because the ability to confer honor depends upon the giver as well as the recipient. (We all know people from whom we would not want to receive honorable recognition.) As Aristotle argued against other concepts, he finally settled on happiness, eudaimonia. Happiness is the end, and not a means toward anything else.

Every action can be traced to an attempt to increase well-being. If I ask you why you want to be rich, the answer usually can be distilled to an attempt to be happy. We never strive to be happy in order to be rich, but often strive to be rich in order to be happy. Happiness is also self-sustaining. If someone is happy, we don't usually ask whether they are also rich or attractive. On the other hand, if someone is rich or famous, we often ask whether they are also happy. Happiness is self-sufficient as an end in itself.

MY PATH TO FLOURISHING

After finishing my residency and fellowship, I was on the typical path of most young doctors. I was excited about my new private practice job and the associated increase in income. I bought a new car, sold our small house in the city, and moved to a larger house in a good suburban school district. All the years of hard work had finally paid off, and I expected to have a dramatic boost in my happiness level.

To everyone around me, I was living the dream. However, I soon became aware of two major problems: my expenses were increasing with my salary, and I wasn't any happier than I had been during other periods in my life. In many ways, my new lifestyle often caused more anxiety and stress. It was at that point that I realized I needed to change my behaviors. I needed to learn different things in order to live a different life.

Despite humanity's near-single-minded drive to achieve happiness and contentment, the majority of people on the planet are far from their eudaimonia. A state of fully realized potential, or dharma, requires insight and a deep connection to your true self. Without this self-awareness, you can't fulfill the fundamental need for meaning and impact. We are all meant to engage in a continuous process of learning, growing, and living well. Unlocking this potential in order to live a more authentic, joyful, and meaningful life can, and must, become our life's work.

There have been some common themes in the steps that I have taken to move closer to my full potential. Perhaps the most fundamental theme is one of self-awareness. In order to gain this insight, I needed to stop living life on autopilot and ask myself some difficult questions. One of the most important habits that helped me to answer these questions was to begin journaling consistently. My journal was a sanctuary where I could freely discuss my worries and perceived failings. There were many days when I could feel a deep unrest inside of me. In the past, I would simply push past this feeling, which would eventually go away. By taking the time to write about it, I discovered that the reason for the unrest was often because I had acted in a way that I knew was not optimal. The inner tension could be related to an uncomfortable interaction at work or an anxiety about a future event that was out of my control. In time, I could occasionally recognize this unrest and resolve it without the need to write about it. Keeping a journal also gave me the space to develop more insight and a broader perspective on important topics that I was learning over the years. I could sketch new ideas and try to put complex concepts into my own words to gain a better understanding of them.

While I wrote extensively on many big-picture questions, there emerged three major questions that helped me explore the gap between my current life and my fully realized potential:

- What am I doing?
- How am I acting?
- Why does it matter?

The first question I asked was "What am I doing?" This has to do with the vision of my place in the world, my unique dharma, my sacred duty. I realized that if we don't know where we want to go, have a firm vision of what we want to be and how we want to be living, then we will just bounce around reacting to various people and circumstances. This was how I often felt in my own life.

When exploring what I was meant to do in this world and trying to answer the larger question of "What am I doing?" I took time to journal on some deeper questions:

- What did I love to do as a child?
- What do I do that doesn't feel like work?
- What would I pay to do?
- If I had $10 million in the bank and had already traveled everywhere that I wanted to go, what would I do each day?

This process took a several months. I forced myself to answer these questions in my journal. When I did, I realized that what I really loved to do was to learn about how to live better. I really enjoyed studying concepts at the intersection of philosophy and psychology that gave me more insight on leading an optimal life. When thinking about my younger years, I had always gravitated toward books that tried to provide answers to the deeper questions of life. I remember reading *The Power of Positive Thinking* by Norman Vincent Peale and *I'm OK—You're OK* by Thomas Harris in high school. On my visits to India as a child, I picked up several books by the well-known Indian philosopher J. Krishnamurti. As I looked around me, I saw many people who had good lives by anyone's standards but were not living the Good Life, one of flourishing or eudaimonia. Instead, there was a lot of anxiety, stress, depression, and generalized discontent. People were functioning but not flourishing, and this included me.

I knew through my reading and learning that there must be a different way to live, and I was determined to find it. I thought about my kids and how I wanted them to learn these principles earlier in life. That deep desire is what drives me to continue to learn. It drove me to write this book. It drives me to teach these principles to a variety of people from students to doctors.

This leads to the second question on my road to fully realized potential: how am I acting?

I realized that it's not enough to have a clear vision of what I want to do if I lie, cheat, and treat people poorly in my effort to fulfill this vision. This will not lead to a life of flourishing. Answering this question when I was younger would have been great. Understanding what virtue meant, and how important concepts like integrity, honesty, and compassion contributed to an overall sense of tranquility certainly would have made my youth better. I struggled mightily in these areas. While I have grown into these virtues, it has not been without significant effort.

The first part of learning to act well was to understand the concept of virtue, defined as "excellence of character." It has become clear to me that there are unshakable principles of effective living that are common across all cultures and time periods. As I read many authors, ranging from Seneca to Stephen Covey, they all preached that living the Good Life is synonymous with developing excellent character traits like integrity, perseverance, gratitude, courage, and service. For me, one very simple way to develop virtue was to adopt the Golden Rule: treat everyone the way I want to be treated. Although this seemed overly simple and even trite, it really worked when I thought about it in the moment of a stressful interaction. If someone interrupted me at work, I could respond more often with patience rather than react with annoyance. Instead of becoming upset at a rude driver, I could empathize that they may be having a bad day.

The second part of acting well was having a clear understanding of what values and behaviors were important to me. What does my ideal self look like?

- Did I want to be calm and patient in the face of stressors, or did I want to overreact at every little inconvenience?
- Did I want to appreciate what I have—health, security, freedom—or did I want to complain about what I didn't have?

- Did I want to treat others how I want to be treated, or just treat them based on how I felt at that moment?
- Did I want to be authentic and honest with people, or simply act the way I thought would make me more popular?
- Did I want to be optimistic and enthusiastic and focus on what was going well, or did I want to get down on myself at the first sign of struggle?

By having this clear vision of my ideal self, I have been able to answer the question "How am I acting?" Of course, many things still upset me, and I'm often far from perfect in my actions, but at least I know how I should be acting.

The final question that I then asked myself was, "Why does it matter?" What difference did I make? To avoid regret later in life, I wanted to face these difficult questions while I still had time. It's commonly said that, on your deathbed, only two things matter:

- Who did you become—did you realize your full potential?
- How many people did you serve? How many lives did you improve?

By answering the first two questions—"What am I doing?" and "How am I acting?"—I could get closer to my unique calling in life and try to perform it with excellent character.

There was one final step on the road to an optimal life: applying these efforts to something larger than myself. The concept of service to others is a common theme among most religious and philosophical texts. Modern psychology has scientifically validated service as a key component to happiness. For me, serving others has never come naturally. What I have come to realize is that an optimal (flourishing) life consists of both purpose (fully realized potential) and meaning (service). I believe that we all have the same purpose in life: to fully realize our potential, our highest self, in what we do and how we act. However, it's not until we use this potential for a cause larger than ourselves that we are able to gain meaning and truly lead an optimal life.

Answering the above questions has certainly brought some clarity and direction to my life. However, there is a big difference between knowing what to do and actually doing it. Intellectually, I often know the correct response or action, but still let my emotions get the better of me. Some say it's like the difference between knowledge and wisdom. Anyone can gain knowledge, but it's not until you apply this knowledge that you will gain wisdom.

Given the importance of achieving happiness, it's surprising how little training we receive in understanding the principles behind well-being. Perhaps even more shocking is how little attention most people pay to what actually makes them happy. Many people live lives filled with anxiety, worry, regret, and discomfort. They don't really understand why their thoughts and actions are not making them happier. They continue to long for the bigger house, new romance, nicer car, or winning lottery ticket to be able to finally be happy. These things may lead to temporary spikes in happiness (defined as a transitory emotional state) but don't contribute significantly to the pursuit of eudaimonia or a flourishing life.

I'm doing fine but don't really feel a lot of joy or fulfillment— isn't there more to life?

To find an answer to this question, and to explore the nature of life itself, the Bhagavad Gita offers us some guidance. Mahatma Gandhi was never without a copy of the Bhagavad Gita. It's rumored that he started each day brushing his teeth and reading at the same time. In his autobiography, Gandhi expressed his love for the text as such:

> When disappointment stares me in the face and all alone I see not one ray of light, I go back to the Bhagavad Gita. I find a verse here and a verse there and I immediately begin to smile in the midst of overwhelming tragedies—and my life has been full of external tragedies—and if they have left no visible, no indelible scar on me, I owe it all to the teaching of Bhagavad Gita.

As a child, I attended the temple and went to Hindu camps, but no one ever mentioned the Bhagavad Gita. I asked my father about his experience with the text. He told me that everyone in India already knows the story, as it's taught to them throughout childhood. I'm sure that I would not have grasped the significance of the Bhagavad Gita had I attempted to read it as a child, but a simplified overview of the story and a few key themes would have offered a useful framework to my developing consciousness.

As a brief overview, the story takes place on a battlefield before the start of the Kurukshetra War and consists of conversations between the warrior prince Arjuna and his charioteer Krishna, the supreme manifestation of the Lord Himself. The war is between two groups of closely related cousin families who are fighting for control of the kingdom. The protagonist, Arjuna, is hesitating before waging battle against his own cousins and uncles. Arjuna faces two right-vs.-right decisions:

1. Should he carry out his individual duty and avoid bloodshed against his own friends and family?
2. Or should he carry out his sacred duty as a warrior and fight for his just cause?

A Western reader might expect God (in this case, Lord Krishna disguised as the charioteer) to convince Arjuna not to kill his own family. Krishna, however, offers different advice and describes the path that each of us can follow by living in harmony with universal laws and order as we seek to live our highest truths. Krishna begins the discussion by reminding Arjuna that the eternal self never perishes. All of us occupy a physical vessel or body, which is temporary, but the essence of our being (our soul) is eternal.

> For the soul, there is neither birth nor death at any time. He has not come into being, does not come into being, and will not come into being. He is unborn, eternal, ever-existing and primeval. He is not slain when the body is slain.

The concept of reincarnation is beyond the scope of this book, but we can understand how this concept of an everlasting nature of being may provide liberation in our current life. One of the challenges we face in Western society is the constant perception of the finite nature of life, the fixed amount of time that we all have as we rush to accumulate things in order to be happy. If our eternal self or soul continues on after we die, whether it's through our children, our service and impact to others, or as part of the universe or nature, we lose the sense of urgency to hurry up and live quickly before time runs out. As Krishna states, this belief in our eternal soul provides freedom for us to act in accordance with our sacred duty.

So how to apply the lessons from the Bhagavad Gita to our

search for the Good Life? Let's explore three key concepts from the text.

CONCEPT #1: FIND YOUR HIGHER PURPOSE

The word "dharma" is one of my favorites, and comes from the Sanskrit *dhri*, which means to hold, support, or bear. The word has many meanings, but "sacred duty" or "highest purpose" is a very useful everyday translation. On a larger scale, the scholar Eknath Easwaran defines dharma as "the essential order of things, an integrity and harmony in the universe and the affairs of life that cannot be disturbed without courting chaos. Thus it means rightness, justice, goodness, purpose rather than chance." In the text, Krishna reminds Arjuna that, as a warrior prince and soldier, his dharma is to fight for justice and protect the kingdom. Arjuna's place in the universe is dependent upon his ability to carry out this duty. Krishna goes on to state that everyone will die or be born, but to relinquish your sacred duty is a fate worse than death for the honorable man. Lord Krishna concludes this brief reference to dharma as one's personal duty by saying, "Now if you do not execute this battle, then, having given up your personal dharma and reputation, you shall incur sin."

We can apply this concept of individual purpose or sacred duty to our own lives. We all have a need to find our reason for being alive. Abraham Maslow states, "Your life's work is to find your life's work." What is your dharma? Are you living your own dharma or following someone else's path? Krishna has some advice for us:

> It is better to strive in one's own dharma than to succeed in the dharma of another. Nothing is ever lost in following one's own dharma. But competition in another's dharma breeds fear and insecurity.

It's important to note that your dharma can and should change over the course of your life. For example, my dharma has ranged from a high school and college student to a karate instructor, radiology resident/fellow, attending radiologist, husband, father, and student/author.

As a student in high school and college, I focused on working to maintain good grades while trying to discover my path in life. I then found my way to martial arts almost by accident and became obsessed with training and competing while rising to an instructor level. In medical school, I was immersed in obtaining the knowledge required to graduate and enter the competitive field of radiology. As I began my career as an attending radiologist, my interest shifted from the subject of radiology to the business of radiology. I began to study the nonclinical aspects of medicine, including financial analytics, hospital/physician contracts, and physician performance management. Today, I'm involved with developing a new model of optimal wellness that integrates key principles of medicine, psychology, neuroscience, and leadership. This is all just to illustrate that my dharma has taken many forms and functions, and each has been as important as the others.

It took several years of study for me to fully understand what my true dharma is. My highest purpose in life has nothing to do with radiology or money or other external indicators of success. My dharma is to create a close-knit family unit filled with love, optimism, gratitude, resilience, purpose, and service. In other words, my reason for living is to achieve a state of eudaimonia for all of us.

Stephen Cope states in *The Great Work of Your Life: A Guide for the Journey to Your True Calling*:

> Dharma is a response to the urgent—though often hidden— need of the moment. Each of us feels some aspect of the world's suffering acutely. It tears at our hearts. Others don't see it or don't care. But we feel it. And we must pay attention. We must act. This little corner of the world is ours to transform. This little corner of the world is ours to save.

CONCEPT #2: DO IT FULLY

If you bring forth what is within you, what you bring forth will save you; if you do not bring forth what is within you, what you do not bring forth will destroy you.

—GNOSTIC GOSPEL OF THOMAS

It's not enough to find our own dharma or highest purpose for living; we must carry out our dharma to the best of our abilities. Whether your dharma is that of a parent, a physician, or a janitor, you must carry out your work with complete effort and deliberate practice.

In his book *Outliers*, Malcolm Gladwell describes the importance of deliberate practice. He argues that success is less about individual genius and more related to circumstances that provide opportunity for an enormous amount of effort. He applies a 10,000-hour rule to the Beatles, who performed live in Hamburg, Germany, 1,200 times over a four-year period. It was during this intensive period of work that the group developed their talents and found their unique sound. Gladwell also describes Bill Gates fulfilling the 10,000-hour rule by having access to a high school computer at the age of thirteen and spending 10,000 hours programming on it. The deliberate practice on a specific task for twenty hours per week for ten years is the key to success in any field—but only if this practice is coupled with the desire to improve. It's not enough to simply put in the time without the goal of mastery or, at the very least, improvement.

Are you fully engaging in deliberate practice? If your dharma is as a teacher, are you engaging in deliberate practice with a desire for constant improvement, or are you simply counting the days until summer vacation? If your dharma is as a physician, are you spending deliberate effort in trying to be the best physician that you can be for the sake of your patients and community, or are you burned out and on autopilot for the money? If your dharma is as a parent, are you learning and practicing evidence-based strategies to raise honest, responsible, resilient, and compassionate kids, or are you simply rushing them from one activity to another to avoid feeling left behind from what others are doing?

Time is too precious and life too fleeting to engage in activities to which we are not fully committed. Spend some time thinking about your dharma or sacred duty at this point in your life. Once you discover this highest purpose, focus on it. Live it. Breathe it. Do it fully!

CONCEPT #3: LET GO OF THE RESULTS

The third concept that Krishna teaches Arjuna is to let go of the results of his actions and turn it over to the higher power. Once you have identified your dharma (in Arjuna's case, as a warrior soldier) and performed your dharma fully (fight to the best of your abilities), you must then let go of the fruits of your labor.

> You should never engage in action for sake of reward, nor should you long for inaction. Perform work in this world, Arjuna, as a man established within himself—without selfish attachments, and alike in success and defeat.

This concept of detachment from results of our actions is a common theme among the stoic philosophers and has had a powerful effect on my own approach to life. I found that the more I pursued activities simply for the process of completing something important, the more successful I became in achieving favorable outcomes. For example, instead of focusing on gaining more hospital contracts (very important for a venture-backed company) or garnering more respect in the radiology community (important for the ego), I shifted my focus toward creating an exceptionally innovative and radiology-friendly group. This practice environment allowed me and my colleagues to develop a new breed of radiologists who were service-oriented, hardworking team players instead of entitled lone wolves. This shift in my attention to the process of creating what I believe is needed, rather than on external results often beyond my control, provided liberation and increased enjoyment in my day-to-day work.

Figure out what you were put on this earth to do, put all of your efforts into doing it, and let go of the results. When implemented correctly, these three steps have the power to change many lives. The steps are often very simple and profound, but difficult to put into practice. It takes time and effort to discover one's dharma. True, it's much easier to float through life on a reactive path, reliant on chance and the influence of others. Deliberate practice and carrying out one's duties to the best of your ability requires discipline and perseverance. However, it yields the most effective and consistent results. It's what allows us to fulfill our dharma and move toward the Good Life.

CHAPTER 2

STOICISM

Stoicism changed my life. It has affected the way I interact with other people (especially my kids), how I view successes and failures, and how I view my place in this world. After reading Marcus Aurelius's *Meditations*, I realized that we are all philosophers, or at least that we all should be. The word "philosopher" is literally translated as a "lover of wisdom" from the Greek words *philos*, "loving", and *sophos*, "wise, a sage." Wisdom in this context refers to the knowledge of life. With this definition, philosophers are people who are in love with learning how to live.

Philosophy offers us a very practical guide to living well. We all need to be philosophers because as we discovered from Aristotle and as we will see with the Stoics, there is no higher goal than to achieve this state of eudaimonia, or living well. In the days of ancient Greece, parents carefully chose schools of philosophy for their children in much the same way we choose colleges today. Parents recognized the importance of philosophy in order to develop a sort of personal code to live the Good Life. Stoicism was the dominant philosophy of the Western world for several hundred years but lost its prominence when the emperor Constantine declared Christianity the official religion of the Roman Empire in the fourth century.

At this point, religion largely supplanted philosophy as a moral compass and means to living a purposeful life. Philosophy morphed from a very useful practical guide for optimal living to esoteric academic principles discussed only among university professors. If we entered a book-store in ancient Greece, the philosophy section would be completely different than it is today. Titles such as *Of Love, Of Human Life*, and *Of Just Dealing* by Epicurus; or *On Anger, On Leisure*, and *Moral Letters* by Seneca; and *Proofs That Pleasure Is Not a Good* by Chrysippus would be displayed prominently. Philosophers in those days asked and answered meaningful questions that offered a path for all to follow. We must return philosophy to its roots and utilize its timeless principles to allow us to learn how to live in this life and in the right way. We must all become philosophers in order for us, our children, and our society to truly flourish. Seneca writes in *Moral Letters*:

Shall I tell you what philosophy holds out to humanity?

Counsel. One person is facing death, another is vexed by poverty, while another is tormented by wealth—whether his own or someone else's; one man is appalled by his misfortunes while another longs to get away from his own prosperity; one man is suffering at the hands of men, another at the hands of the Gods...All mankind is stretching out their hands to you on every side. Lives that have been ruined, lives that are on the way to ruin are appealing for some help; it is to you that they look for hope and assistance... Philosophy takes as her aim the state of happiness...She shows us what are real and what are only apparent evils. She strips men's minds of empty thinking, bestows a greatness that is solid, and administers a check to greatness where it is puffed up and all an empty show; she sees that we are left no doubt about the difference between what is great and what is bloated.

As I read these lines for the first time on my journey through Stoicism, I realized that there is no greater knowledge to teach my children than this aim that Seneca describes.

STOICISM: A BRIEF HISTORY

Stoic philosophy was founded by Zeno of Citium (a part of Cyprus) around 300 BC. Zeno taught his philosophy in public at the Stoa Poikile (painted porch), giving rise to the name Stoicism. As in all of early Greek ethics, happiness or eudaimonia is the ultimate goal in life for Stoicism.

Unlike Christianity, the focus in Stoic philosophy is on living well in this life rather than trying to prepare for an afterlife. Stoicism reemerged as a popular philosophy in the Renaissance when people returned to reason rather than faith to find answers on how to live. I focused on the texts and principles from late (Roman) Stoics; namely, Seneca, Epictetus, and Marcus Aurelius.

One of the most fascinating aspects of Stoicism is the simplicity and accessibility of its core precepts. For the Stoics, tranquility or equanimity were available to everyone to achieve. It was not, however, easy to attain. It required daily and deliberate practice in areas of reason, logic, mindfulness, self-awareness, and self-control. The Stoics believed that the universe is governed by absolute law or cosmic order and that the essential nature of human beings is reason. To live according to nature means that man should conform his actions to the larger universal order while acting in accordance with his own nature: reason. Living according to nature has profound implications for us as we attempt to live a life of joy and purpose.

VIRTUE, VICE, AND THE REST OF THE WORLD

A good character is the only guarantee of everlasting, carefree happiness.

—SENECA, *LETTERS FROM A STOIC*

For me, the concept of virtue defined as "excellence of character" is key to understanding the Stoic path toward the Good Life. Similar to Aristotle, this "good life" was one of eudaimonia, found by living a life of virtue. Stoic theory describes virtue (*arete*, excellence in character) as the only good thing and vice, its opposite, as the only bad thing. Everything else in life is considered indifferent (not considered good nor bad). What most of us consider good (wealth, status, material goods, even health) are not needed for the Stoics to live well. All that is required is living a virtuous life. The indifferent things, although worth pursuing to the extent that it is appropriate for humans to seek food, shelter, companionship, and pleasure, are in no way required for eudaimonia. As we explore the concept of the indifferent things, we have to accept that what is good must benefit us unconditionally. By using this standard, we can understand how conventional pursuits such as wealth or status will not pass this test. A wealthy person can, for example, use their wealth for harmful ends. By classifying these concepts as indifferent, the Stoics are merely saying they are not needed for well-being and are neither good nor bad. They don't believe that we can live entirely without some of these things. In fact, they go on to classify indifferents into preferred indifferents which include things like health, strength, wealth, beauty, and reputation. It's preferable to have these things only if we have the knowledge and wisdom to act virtuously in the pursuit of them and to realize that they are not needed for our happiness.

For the Stoics, the way to achieve a happy or flourishing life is to live virtuously (excellence in character). Instead of an abstract notion of virtue, the Stoics produced a classification of four primary virtues, as listed by John Stobeaus:

- Prudence: (concerns appropriate acts) knowledge of what one is to do and not to do and what is neither
- Temperance: (concerning human impulses) knowledge of what is to be chosen and avoided and what is neither
- Justice: (concerning distributions) knowledge of the distribution of proper value to each person
- Courage: (concerning standing firm) knowledge of what is terrible and what is not terrible and what is neither

A modern interpretation of these main virtues might be:

- We must act with self-restraint in all circumstances.
- We must choose our activities carefully and carry them out wisely.
- We must be fair to others.
- We must face difficult circumstances with courage.

If we can live this way and only if we live this way, can we live well. Nothing else is needed for our ability to fully flourish.

How do these principles apply to us? Most of us pursue worthwhile goals such as getting an education, earning an income, falling in love, and raising children. Both Seneca and Marcus Aurelius were extremely wealthy with high status in their communities. We must make a distinction between the way we pursue our goals from the goals themselves. In other words, our goals are really indifferent, but the way we act to achieve them is *vitally important* and requires us to act with excellent character (virtuously). If we adopt this mindset, we can treat setbacks and failures as harming our goals, but not ourselves. As long as we continue to act toward perfecting our moral character, we have not been harmed. This highlights the concept of what is truly our own and our need to focus on what we can control, specifically, our ability to act wisely with self-restraint and to be fair and courageous. Marcus Aurelius sums it up very nicely in *Meditations* when he says:

> You take things you don't control and define them as "good" or "bad." And so of course when the "bad" things happen, or the "good" ones don't, you blame the Gods and feel hatred for the people responsible—or those you decide to make responsible. Much of our bad behavior stems from trying to apply those criteria. If we limited "good" and "bad" to our own actions, we'd have no call to challenge God, or to treat other people as enemies.

THE POWER OF FOCUSING ON OUR POWER

There are things which are within our power, and there are things which are beyond our power. Within our power are opinion, aim, desire, aversion and in a word, whatever affairs are our own. Beyond our power are body, property, reputation, office, and in one word, whatever are not properly our own affairs.

—EPICTETUS, *ENCHIRIDION*

Epictetus refers to the concept of volition, which will be further elaborated upon later in this book when discussing Sonya Lyubormirsky's formula for happiness. By focusing on our voluntary thoughts and actions to the best of our ability, we will have achieved success, according to the Stoics, regardless of the external results. We can only attain tranquility (according to Epictetus) if we focus on things within our control (our actions, efforts, and behaviors) and disregard all things out of our control (results, opinions of others, social status). We need to focus on what is under our control—what we think about, how hard we work, how we respond to setbacks, what goals we choose to pursue, and how we treat others. The death of a loved one or the loss of a job is beyond our control. We can't control a rude driver cutting us off on the road or our child striking out with bases loaded and the game on the line. We can only choose our response and we must choose our optimal response. We can't control if we get sick, but we can control our diet and exercise. We can't control if our child doesn't perform well in a sporting event; we can only control our efforts to teach the importance of practice. This detachment from the results and focus on the process helps us focus on dharma (choose our activity), do it fully (courageously), and let go of the results (indifference).

The Stoics believed that the universe is a rational place with a predestined cosmic order, and that man is a rational being capable of the use of reason. Seneca described virtue as being "nothing else than right reason." For the Stoics, the ability to distinguish between what we can and cannot control, to live life virtuously and in accordance with nature, requires the use of reason, discipline, and daily practice. Reason can guide us in choosing which activities to pursue while virtue can guide us in how we pursue them.

The common misconception that Stoics don't have any emotions arises from the belief that emotions are based on judgment. We will all experience emotional reactions to events that cause anger, fear, and despair, but after the initial instinctive emotional reaction, it's our reason or judgment that determines our response and ultimate happiness with the event. Reason provides an ability to appropriately judge an event and choose our optimal response. This does not imply that we must suppress our emotions. In fact, the full acceptance of a negative emotion is felt to be critical in the ability to also experience joy. Tal Ben-Shahar calls this the "permission to be human."

As we face daily challenges of life, it's critical for us to realize that it's not the event that creates the response, but it's how we interpret the event that determines everything. The response to the situation becomes the situation. Marcus Aurelius states, "Take away the complaint, 'I have been harmed,' and the harm is taken away" (*Meditations* 4.7). "Tranquility comes when you stop caring what they say. Or think, or do. Only what you do." (*Meditations* 4.18). Finally, in one of my favorite books by Ayn Rand, *The Fountainhead*, when asked by the novel's antagonist, "What do you think of me?" Howard Roark replies simply, "I don't."

SPIRITUAL EXERCISES AND DELIBERATE PRACTICE: LIFE IS EASY IF YOU LIVE IT THE HARD WAY, AND LIFE IS HARD IF YOU LIVE IT THE EASY WAY

The habits of your thoughts will become the character of your mind; for the soul is dyed by the thoughts. Dye it, then, with thoughts such as these; wherever one lives, one can live well—even if he must live in a palace.

—MARCUS AURELIUS, *MEDITATIONS*

Socrates said, "To know good is to do good," but for most

of us, this simply is not true. We all know that we should eat more vegetables, exercise more, spend more quality time with our family, worry less about what others think, remain calm when events are out of our control, and watch less TV. We know we shouldn't sign up for another travel team or structured activity yet do so out of fear of our child being left behind. We realize that eight-year-olds are probably too young for sleepover parties but don't want to risk our child not being popular. We understand that a thirteen-year-old child's self-worth does not depend upon his batting average, yet we tend to dismiss the poor hitters as somehow inferior children. Putting what we know into practice is difficult and requires us to develop rituals and habits. One of the concepts that we can borrow from most religious practices is the use of rituals. Each service within a specific religion follows a routine so that each time you go to mass, you essentially repeat the same sequence of prayers. I urge you to follow this same principle with ideas and concepts in this book that resonate with you—it's the only way to put them into practice. I have tried many different forms of journaling, meditation practices, and visualization techniques at different times of the day and for various lengths of time. It's trial and error, but the ritual of the practice must be established.

JOURNALING

We read about Gandhi starting each day brushing his teeth

while reading the Bhagavad Gita. The Stoic philosophers Seneca, Epictetus, and Marcus Aurelius also practiced and applied their principles to daily living. In his *Meditations*, Marcus Aurelius remarks:

> When you wake up in the morning, tell yourself, "The people I deal with today will be meddling, ungrateful, arrogant, dishonest, jealous, and surly. They are like this because they can't tell good from evil. But I have seen the beauty of good, and the ugliness of evil, and have recognized that the wrongdoer has a nature related to my own—not of the same blood or birth, but the same mind, and possessing a share of the divine. And so none of them can hurt me. No one can implicate me in ugliness. Nor can I feel angry at my relative, or hate him. We were born to work together like feet, hands, and eyes, like the two rows of teeth, upper and lower. To obstruct each other is unnatural. To feel anger at someone, to turn your back on him: these are obstructions."

Aurelius, the most powerful man on earth, was expressing daily reminders of compassion and service. He believed that we are all connected with each other and with the universe. Each of us has a duty to live our lives to the best of our ability in the service of others and to the larger cosmic order.

Seneca claimed to have a daily practice of recounting the day's events and judging his actions according to his own virtues. We can do a similar practice by keeping a daily journal, recalling the events of the day in detail from the moment you wake up to the present moment. Remember every interaction, every response, and how you performed according to your best self—your virtuous self. Write it all down and visualize how you would act differently next time.

This journaling practice has dramatically affected my life. I have been able to ruminate less about things that I wish I had handled differently. By writing down these events and visualizing them positively, I have also gained clarity and a small sense of space between the stimulus (event) and my (optimal) response. In other cases, by writing about times that I acted with integrity, honesty, and compassion, I have been able to reinforce these positive actions that can become more habitual. The next time you have a less than favorable interaction with your spouse, child, friend, or colleague, write it down and visualize how you would handle it next time (for there will always be a next time).

THE POWER OF NEGATIVE VISUALIZATION: IMAGINE IT ALL GONE

Another practice that I borrowed from both Marcus Aurelius and Epictetus is negative visualization. A powerful force in human nature is the concept of hedonic adaptation, which simply states that we quickly adapt and take for granted the positive events or people in our lives. One way to avoid this adaptation is to think and really visualize how you would feel if you no longer had a job, your wife had left, or your child was sick. How would I feel if I found out I had cancer or that this was the last day of my life? Would I care about the minor inconveniences of life, or would I smile and make sure that those I cared about knew how I felt?

If the kids are running around screaming and yelling, imagine if they were no longer living with you or were not healthy enough to play. I believe that negative visualization is the antidote to hedonic adaptation and to the entitlement mindset that is so pervasive in our society and especially in our children. Each of us should spend one minute each day visualizing that something that is dear to us—our family, health, friends, job, house, or other possessions—has been taken away. Really imagining life without one of these precious things is the key to really appreciating them. Contrary to what may seem like a morose practice, visualizing yourself without all of the good things in your life brings both gratitude and mindfulness that are key components of happiness.

ACCEPT, THEN ACT

Finally, a third Stoic exercise is to accept each moment as if it were meant to happen. This is based on the Stoic belief in fatalistic determinism—that things are predestined according to the universal order. Without getting into the merits of that argument, this concept of active acceptance of each moment is very powerful. It does not imply that things happen for the best, but it does allow us to make the best of what is happening in the moment.

Eckhart Tolle elaborates on this concept in his book *The Power of Now*. He advises us to act as if we had chosen the event to happen exactly as it has and choose our best response. A mantra that I have used is "I chose this moment, and I'll choose my optimal response." When my daughter is having a meltdown at the end of the day, instead of yelling back at her (which still does happen), I can act as if I chose her meltdown to happen. It doesn't make the meltdown go away, but it does create a tiny space before my instinctual angry response. This space allows me to better act according to my own nature—through the use of reason and with virtue. Let us accept and then act well rather than complain and act out.

FINAL THOUGHTS FROM ARISTOTLE, THE BHAGAVAD GITA, AND THE STOICS

The pursuit of human flourishing was (and still is) the ultimate goal for human life. This state of eudaimonia can be achieved by identifying and embracing our duty in life, performing this duty with our highest character and best effort without attachment to the results or other external events beyond our control. This will be our contribution to the larger universe—whether that is God, nature, or cosmic order—and will provide each of us with a life well lived.

PART II

THE PRESENT

LESSONS FROM POSITIVE PSYCHOLOGY

CHAPTER 3

INSIDE, NOT OUTSIDE

Question: I keep signing my kids up for teams, activities, and private lessons so they won't be left behind or feel left out. Don't they need to be successful in order to be happy?

Answer: Focus on intrinsic character development, not extrinsic social standing.

Parents have been sold a lie. We have been made to feel guilty if our child feels the slightest amount of adversity. We try to remove every obstacle from their path, not wanting to upset them. We have been made to feel that our self-worth and the self-worth of our kids depend on their athletic performance or popularity. We find the most insecure parents boasting about their child's batting average or what exclusive party their kids were invited to attend.

We have been told that material or academic success will lead to happiness, so we teach our kids that extrinsic results, not intrinsic effort and character, are what matter in life. They understand very quickly that getting an A is more important than really learning the material. They focus on achieving more money, more titles, and more accolades in an effort to become happier. We want to move from being parents of gifted children to becoming gifted parents, so we have parents arguing with teachers to place their children in the honors program.

We believe in these myths because, ultimately, we want our children to be happy. This makes sense given the strong benefits associated with happiness. Happy people are more likely to get married and have strong relationships. They achieve greater success in their careers and earning potential. They live longer and have a higher quality of life. In other words, happy people lead the Good Life. This is the reason that ancient philosophers viewed happiness as the ultimate goal in life—the end in itself. It's clear that happiness leads to greater success in love, work, and health. But the reverse is not necessarily true. Getting married or making more money does not automatically make us happier. The same is true for our children. Focusing on achieving external indicators of success such as popularity or athletic performance will not automatically lead to happier kids. Neither will satisfying their every desire or creating a life devoid of struggle.

While happiness often leads to success, success does not always lead to happiness.

It's important to remember to view happiness more as flourishing (eudaimonia) than as a transient emotional state that can fluctuate on a daily basis. We discussed this concept of happiness and flourishing in earlier chapters. Fortunately for us, there is a growing field studying the science of happiness (flourishing)—positive psychology. We can now combine modern, evidence-based scientific principles from positive psychology with ancient wisdom from philosophy to form a coherent guide for daily living. This guide can function as a touchstone to help guide us to better choices. Should we sign up for that travel team that eliminates quality family time? Should we praise our kids for being smart or athletic instead of for their effort? Should we avoid trying something new that may cause us to fail? Do we teach our kids to fit in to avoid being labeled as weird? These are the landmines of childhood that will shape the lives of our children and all of our lives.

THE HISTORY OF POSITIVE PSYCHOLOGY

Before WWII, psychology had three distinct missions: cure mental illness, make lives of all people better, and identify/ nurture high talent.

—MARTY SELIGMAN

The National Institute of Mental Health changed the course of psychology after World War II. Psychologists could now earn a comfortable living by researching and treating mental illness. As a result, there have been tremendous advancements in the treatment of mental illness over the past fifty years. At least fourteen disorders that were previously intractable can now be cured or considerably relieved. As a physician, the rigorous disease modeling approach of the Diagnostic and Statistical Manual (DSM) makes a lot of sense.

Unfortunately, this focus on pathology left behind the other two goals of psychology—improve the lives of all people and study genius. In the 1950s, humanistic thinkers such as Carl Rogers, Erich Fromm, and Abraham Maslow revived interest in these areas of psychology by creating therapeutic models that supported individual happiness and self-actualization. Many psychologists have been critical of the humanistic movement; they assert that it lacks scientific rigor. The field of positive psychology combined the focus of the humanistic thinkers on individual potential with the scientific methods of traditional psychology. Positive psychology officially began as a new area of psychology in 1998 when Martin Seligman (considered by many to be the father of positive psychology) chose it as the theme for his term as president of the American Psychological Association.

POSITIVE PSYCHOLOGY

Positive psychology focuses on human flourishing rather than alleviating distress. Traditional psychology focused on pathology—on a person that is functioning at a -8 and moving them to a 0 or +1. Positive psychology, on the other hand, focuses on the person who is functioning at a +1 and improving them to a +8 on a scale of human flourishing. We need both areas of focus. For too long we have been content to simply get by or exist. As long as someone is functioning and not in acute distress, we as a society feel they are OK. In reality, there is unrealized joy and potential within all of us. We need proven techniques to unlock this potential and really flourish in the short time we all have in life.

A MODEL OF HAPPINESS

Positive psychology takes you through the countryside of pleasure and gratification, up into the high country of strength and virtue, and finally to the peaks of lasting fulfillment: meaning and purpose.

—MARTY SELIGMAN

According to Seligman, we can experience three kinds of happiness:

- Pleasure and gratification
- Embodiment of strengths and virtues
- Meaning and purpose

Each kind of happiness is linked to positive emotion, but from his quote, there is a progression from the first type of happiness of pleasure/gratification to strengths and virtues and finally to meaning and purpose.

He describes each stage as the Pleasant, Good, and Meaningful Life. The Pleasant Life is one of pleasure, in which our basic bodily needs are met. This is the hedonistic stage of satisfying our cravings for food, drink, sex, and toys. As we know from hedonic adaptation, this is a treadmill that requires more intense pleasures that never ultimately satisfy us.

The Good Life, according to Seligman, is one in which our strengths and virtues are cultivated every day as we seek to fulfill our unique potential. This was the focus of ancient philosophers who believed that a life of virtue and duty were key components of human flourishing. This concept of unique potential was also well articulated as dharma (sacred duty) in the Bhagavad Gita.

The Meaningful Life is one in which we apply our fully developed unique potential for a purpose larger than ourselves. The principles of service to others and a feeling of connection with the universe have been preached by several religious and philosophical texts as universal truths. When we become our highest and best self in order to contribute to others in a meaningful way, we have entered the Meaningful Life.

There are many different models for human flourishing and happiness. Even Dr. Seligman has since updated his Three Dimensions of Happiness Model. The point is not to search for one right definition, but to understand the key components that form the basis of all models. For me, it's the simplicity of Seligman's model that has been critical to explain much of the discontent that many people feel. They search for pleasures and positive emotions, but don't realize that unless you move past this hedonistic stage and cultivate your strengths for some meaningful purpose and develop your best self to make an impact, you'll keep feeling anxious and deeply unfulfilled.

Most people have no problem living in the Pleasant Life; in fact, much of society is firmly rooted in this stage. It's very common for our younger years to be filled with hedonistic pursuits. We may chase money, sex, and possessions. As we get older, we begin searching for the point of it all. We begin to ask ourselves if this is all there is to life. We may feel a growing sense of anxiety and discontent. If we have kids, we may look to them to provide us with meaning. Their success becomes our success. Their academic or athletic achievements are a direct reflection of us. Their popularity is our popularity. Our self-worth is based on their self-worth. We try to fill our hole of discontent with our kids' contentment. This doesn't work. It's the reason we have parents screaming at their kids, coaches, and umpires at sporting events. It's the reason that seven-year-olds have private coaches to get an early edge on their teammates. It's the reason that the term "helicopter parent"—one who is constantly hovering over their child to ensure maximum output—was invented. It's the reason that every parent feels their child should be in the advanced class at school. It's the reason that many kids are urged to get in with the popular crowd, leaving a good but uncool friend behind.

If we understand the need to progress from the Pleasant Life to the Good Life, we can clearly see the source of our misguided pursuits. The reason for our discontent is a growing sense of a deep and unrealized potential. As we are stuck in the Pleasant Life, we are not fully developing our best self. We are not living in harmony with our unique strengths and virtues each day. In short, we can only enter the Good Life by focusing on our own development—our personal growth. This does not mean that we need to live an egocentric life where our own needs are placed above those of our children. Service, compassion, and love are virtues that are important to our highest character. As parents, our main goal is to help guide our children to develop their character and reach their potential. But until we work on ourselves first, we run the risk of trying to realize our own full potential through the potential of our children. If we don't focus on developing our own character and living in harmony with our virtues, we are in no position to teach our kids to live this way. Many parents of the most "successful" kids still feel anxious or unhappy because they don't focus on their own growth and success.

How do we realize our full potential and satisfy the discontent that many of us feel? The doorway to the Good Life begins with a focus on character. The Stoics believed that the only thing required to achieving happiness (flourishing) was to live a life of virtue (excellence in character). Stephen Covey in his book *The Seven Habits of Highly Effective People* states:

> Much of the literature of the first 150 years or so focused on what could be called the Character Ethic as the foundation of success—things like integrity, humility, fidelity, temperance, courage, justice, patience, industry, simplicity, modesty, and the Golden Rule...The Character Ethic taught that there are basic principles of effective living, and that people can only experience true success and enduring happiness as they learn and integrate these principles into their basic character.

There are several aspects of good character that can be developed with the right amount of focus and practice. Gratitude, resilience, optimism, integrity, compassion, and service have all been correlated with improved well-being. These can be exercised on a daily basis to grow the muscles of our character. We are often faced with having to make difficult choices for how we spend our time. We often ask ourselves what is the best approach for raising our children? The correct path is usually the one that leads to the practice of virtue and improvement of character. There may be nothing wrong with joining a travel sports team if it's done for the right reason. Are we joining a more competitive team so our child can improve their skills and learn the link between effort and results (resiliency)? Or are we joining so that we can tell others that our child made the A team?

ADVERSITY IS UNDERRATED

I grew up thinking, like many others, that nirvana or a state of bliss is free of challenges and struggles. We work hard while we are young so we can retire and sit on a beach when we are older. Unfortunately, many recently retired people that left successful and rewarding careers often become bored and depressed in their new "blissful" state. Society has misled us into pursuing a hedonistic lifestyle built on maximizing pleasure at the expense of purpose. Ancient philosophers and modern researchers have proclaimed that hedonism is not the right path to happiness. This is proven every day by the miserable, unhappy lives of many famous movie stars. In fact, you may know many people that are wealthy but not that happy. We have an innate need for a challenge—a need to find meaningful work. This challenge has to have an optimal level of difficulty that matches one's skill level in order to increase our well-being. Too much challenge for the level of ability results in anxiety, discomfort, and frustration. On the other hand, too little stress for the ability level can cause boredom, depression, and unhappiness. Perhaps even worse, this lack of adequate challenge very often results in the creation of stress or worry on trivial matters in an effort to fill this intrinsic need.

For many of us, life has simply become too easy. We consume far more calories than we expend on a daily basis. We spend more time watching television than we do in actual conversations with our family or in reading books. We outsource our food to restaurants. We outsource our physical labor to contractors and lawn care companies. We outsource our kids to teachers and coaches. We outsource our money to financial planners. Most of us spend the majority of our days either sleeping or sitting behind a desk. We don't have much to complain or worry about. And yet we still do. I'm not suggesting that we all return to farms to grow all of our food and work from sunrise to sunset (although I am attracted to the simplicity and effort of that type of lifestyle). What I am suggesting, however, is that we all try to find a little more adversity and challenge in our daily lives. Let's not try to satisfy our every whim.

Let's not fear every little bit of discomfort. Let's not desire a struggle-free existence. Let's not try to protect our kids from ever feeling sad, disappointed, or angry. Struggles are important for all of us to experience. Think back to your own life and the most rewarding experiences. It's very likely that these experiences occurred after some period of adversity or challenge. Kids, in particular, need to learn to deal with loss, struggle, and setbacks. If they have everything given to them, they have no sense of achievement or gratitude. Not only does this prevent them from becoming resilient, it causes them to be unhappy. This "underprivilege of privilege" is an epidemic among upper middle class and wealthy families. Interestingly, studies have shown that affluent kids have less feelings of being in the zone, or flow, in their lives (which correlates with happiness) mainly because of too many structured activities, not enough challenge, and less quality time with parents.

To better understand the relationship between struggles and ultimate happiness, we need to explore the concept of grit. Grit, defined as firmness of mind and spirit in the face of hardship, is strongly correlated with achievement, purpose, and happiness. Research at the Character Lab founded by Angela Duckworth at the University of Pennsylvania's Positive Psychology Center has established the predictive power of grit, over and beyond measures of talent, for objectively measured success outcomes.

For instance, in prospective longitudinal studies, grit predicts surviving the arduous first summer of training at West Point, reaching the final rounds of the National Spelling Bee, retention in the US Special Forces, and graduation from Chicago public high schools, over and beyond domain-relevant talent measures, such as IQ, SAT, or standardized achievement test scores and physical fitness. In multiple studies, grit correlates with lifetime educational attainment and, inversely, lifetime career changes, and divorce. Given the importance of grit in the ultimate success of our children, we need to use adversity as opportunities to develop grit in ourselves and our children. We can create challenges (and struggles) through "stretch" goals for ourselves and our children. These are goals that have a 50 percent chance of success. Collins and Porras introduce the concept of big hairy audacious goals (BHAG) in their book *Built to Last* (113). What is your BHAG? Do you want to write a book? Do you want to raise your batting average to .400? Are you trying to become a starter on the team? Do you want to go back to school to start a new career? We all need these goals. They teach us how to live with a purpose. They teach us how to fail and keep going. They make us more resilient. Ultimately, they make us happier. For many families, the creation of these types of goals can introduce adversity into our children's lives. We need to stop trying to prepare the path for the child but, rather, to start to prepare the child for the path (however rocky that may be). Often, life provides an additional amount of struggle and challenge, whether it's dealing with a friend no longer being nice, missing the game-winning shot, or studying and not getting the A. These daily experiences are also important to the self-esteem, resilience, and happiness of our kids. We need to reframe these obstacles as opportunities for growth. We need to stop trying to run from them but, instead, run toward them—face them head on with a cool head and a compassionate heart. These obstacles are the way forward, so embrace them, become grittier, and remember that adversity is underrated.

PRAISE EFFORT, NOT TALENT: A PRIMER ON THE IMPORTANCE OF MINDSET

By continually focusing on the effort and not the outcome, we can develop what Carol Dweck in her great book *Mindset: The New Psychology of Success* terms as the "growth mindset." This mindset has the belief that most of our basic abilities can be improved through hard work and that the strongest contributor to success is effort and persistence. The growth mindset emphasizes developing intelligence and talent. On the other hand, the fixed mindset places an emphasis on documenting intelligence and talent based on the belief that our basic abilities are fixed traits that cannot be changed and that inherent talent is the main component of success in life. Professor Dweck describes a research study in which students of similar abilities worked on ten problems. These students were then divided into two groups. The first group (fixed mindset) was told, "You got a really good score and must really be smart at this." The second group (growth mindset) was told, "You got a really good score. You must have worked really hard." The fixed mindset group subsequently chose *not* to work on a harder set of problems, and when asked to try them anyway, they performed worse, enjoyed it less, and were more prone to lie about their results. On the other hand, more of the growth mindset group chose to work on harder problems, and while working on these problems, they were more likely to perform better and enjoy the process compared with the first group. They also were less likely to lie about their scores.

The concept of focusing on efforts and not results has dramatically changed our parenting style. In our society, there has been a focus to improve the self-esteem of our children. We attempt this by not keeping score at sporting events to avoid having winners and losers, handing out participation trophies so that no one feels left out, and praising every little achievement no matter how small or easy in order for our kids to feel good about themselves. What this research on mindset demonstrates is that by praising qualities like intelligence or athleticism instead of effort or practice, we are inadvertently sabotaging our children's ability to try new things, take risks, and learn from failure and new experiences. In an environment that praises inherent God-given talent (nothing that the child has done on their own to become smart or athletic), children learn to see life as a series of risky tests that are to be avoided in order to maintain their documented talent. The next time your child brings home a good report card, praise him or her on the effort expended in studying and working hard rather than how smart in math or what a gifted writer he or she must be. The next time that your child plays a great game, instead of telling them what a great athlete he or she is, say that the practice, exercise, and good eating habits seem to really be making a difference.

HOW TO DO MEANINGFUL WORK: FINDING PURPOSE IN YOUR PURPOSE

As we move from the Pleasant Life to the Good Life with a focus on our character development and unique potential, we enter the Meaningful Life by using this potential for a purpose larger than ourselves.

We all want to make an impact. We want to do something important. We want our lives to mean something. We want to live to our full potential. We want to look back on our deathbed with no regrets, having lived a complete life of meaning and joy. How do we do this? Where do we start? There is no shortage of self-help books and life coaches telling us to think positively and to follow our dreams.

While I'm a firm believer in an optimistic attitude, I believe this is often very dangerous advice. These admonitions to find your perfect job can lead to the opposite effect—a life filled with constant discontent, devoid of any real meaning and impact. In order to avoid this trap, we need to look carefully at the relationship between the three Ps: purpose, passion, and practice.

How important is it to have a strong sense of purpose? Is our personal goal of raising great kids enough, or do we need to find meaning and purpose in our professional lives as well? Evidence-based research in positive psychology is confirming what ancient wisdom and religion have been teaching for years: people with a strong sense of purpose are happier, live better, and live longer. Specifically, this sense of purpose is associated with increased optimism, resiliency, well-being, and longevity. A 2014 study titled "Purpose in Life as a Predictor of Mortality across Adulthood" examined data from the longitudinal midlife in the US (MIDUS) sample for six thousand participants over a fourteen-year period. Five hundred eighty-nine participants had died (9 percent) over the follow-up period. Those who died had previously reported a lower sense of purpose and fewer positive relations than did the survivors. Authors Patrick Hill and Nicholas Turiano conclude:

> Purposeful individuals lived longer than their counterparts...
> even when controlling for other markers of psychological

and affective well-being. Moreover, these longevity benefits did not appear to be conditional on the participant's age, how long they lived during the follow-up period, or whether they had retired from the workforce. In other words, having a purpose in life appears to widely buffer against mortality risk across the adult years.

Given the importance of purpose in our quest to lead better and longer lives, we need to clearly understand how to develop it. This understanding relies on dissecting the relationship of passion and practice with purpose.

There are many diverging theories on the best way to develop a sense of purpose in life. Do we find our purpose from our passions—do we only get good at something that we like to do? Conversely, does our sense of purpose arise from our practice—do we get really good at something first and then find meaning from our expertise?

These are important questions to answer. The ability to create meaningful and great work from a strong sense of purpose—the kind that gets you jumping out of bed in the morning—is crucial to leading a meaningful and great life. It turns out that two key components of this type of work are impact and control. Think of people that you know who are leading truly successful (good) lives. I'm referring to the type of lives that are filled with enough wealth, close relationships, work/life balance, service, and personal and spiritual growth. Chances are that they have developed careers that offer a certain amount of control in how they spend their time (and money) while delivering a substantial amount of value and impact to the world around them. How do we find these great jobs and valuable careers? How do our passions contribute to this search?

Cal Newport explores this very question in his excellent book *So Good They Can't Ignore You*. The title of the book is from a famous response that Steve Martin gives when answering frequent questions about what made him successful. In this book, Newport debunks the "passion hypothesis" that is so prevalent in our society today. This hypothesis states that "the key to occupational happiness is to first figure out what you are passionate about and then find a job that matches this passion."

Newport's most famous example is Steve Jobs, the founder of Apple. Jobs promoted the passion hypothesis in his famous commencement speech in 2005 at Stanford when he implored the graduating class "to find what you love to do because that is the only way to do great work." Unfortunately, this advice is misleading. If, as Newport states, Jobs had followed his initial passion, he may have been teaching Zen Buddhism and leading meditation retreats in India. Instead, he learned to become passionate about what he became good at doing. This work became his life's purpose or his life's task and enabled him to create a meaningful and lasting legacy. Viewing Jobs's story in this way leads to more interesting questions: How can we find work that we will eventually love to do? How do we find purpose and meaning in that work to be able to create a great life?

Newport goes on to discuss the concept of "career capital," which I find very helpful in answering the above questions. Great careers (and lives) that provide purpose, impact, control, autonomy, and wealth are both rare and valuable. In order to get these types of jobs, you must be able to trade equally rare and valuable skills. Newport refers to these skills as "career capital," which can be developed and traded throughout one's life for more professional and personal satisfaction. Others have described this capital as "deliberate practice" from the famous 10,000-hour rule developed by Anders Erikkson (and later expanded upon by Malcolm Gladwell) or "mastery" as discussed by Robert Greene in his book *Mastery*. Whatever term you apply, the concept is the same. You need to become really good—world-class—in a particular field. You can then trade this rare and valuable expertise for more control and impact (which are also rare and valuable) as you move throughout your professional career. This is where the relationship between purpose and practice is important to understand.

Throughout history, we have countless examples of successful individuals completing years of intense practice. This practice may have been developed in a formal apprenticeship in the printing business, as in the case of Benjamin Franklin, or in the informal music clubs of Germany, as in the case of the Beatles that we discussed earlier. The story of Benjamin Franklin is illustrative. In his autobiography, he describes that he desperately wanted to be a writer. Against his father's wishes for him to continue the family candle-making business, Franklin signed up for a longer apprenticeship in his older brother's new printing business. Although this would entail harder work and longer hours, Franklin would have access to new books and would learn to develop his own writing style by reading the work of established writers. Through his hard work and focus on his goal of becoming a better writer, Franklin turned an otherwise grueling nine years into an apprenticeship for writing while learning the printing business as well. The critical concept in this and other examples of mastery is a love of learning combined with a strong desire to get better. All of these individuals tried to learn as much as possible in order to become the best in their field. This type of practice should be done at all times in one's life. The ability to immerse yourself in whatever job you happen to be doing will build skills that most can only attribute to talent or luck.

When I was in my radiology residency, it became clear that the ability to perform research was an important and fairly rare attribute in a successful young physician. It required extra time and effort in an already busy period of work. I came to work early, stayed late, and worked on the projects over the weekends. I read countless research articles, learned how to design and conduct experiments, and perhaps most importantly, was able to develop a coherent writing style to publish my results. It's important to note that I did not arrive in residency with a burning desire (passion) to perform research. Once in that setting, I recognized that skill to be valuable, immersed myself in learning how to do it well, and in the process, was able to differentiate myself from other radiology residents. There were two unexpected results from my research experience. I actually learned to enjoy the process and felt that I was contributing to the field of radiology in my small way. Secondly, this differentiation led me to opportunities that I could not have predicted. I was viewed as one of the leaders in my class, elected as chief resident, allowed to tailor a unique combined residency/fellowship track, and offered a faculty position. In other words, I had built career capital which I was able to trade for more professional satisfaction. I repeated this same process while in my first private practice job but replaced research with learning the business of radiology (an equally rare and valuable attribute). These business skills allowed me to be viewed as one of the leaders of my group, to be elected to our executive committee, and eventually to be recruited as a physician executive to a radiology startup company.

Everywhere you turn, there are articles or coaches telling you to stop wasting your life, quit your job, and go follow your dreams to do what you love to do. This is good advice if your current job is harmful to other individuals or society in general. Most people, however, have jobs that are not evil, but are often difficult and tedious. The answer is not to keep searching for that perfect job that provides endless hours of flow and never seems like work. This constant searching leads to unhappiness since producing anything of value will always require effort.

What is not as popular for career and life coaches to proclaim is the following answer to people looking for more meaningful work:

- Whatever work you find yourself doing, do it better than anyone else.
- Always give your best effort.
- Learn more about your business than others know.
- Invest in your personal and professional growth.
- Become indispensable. Keep your word. Don't cheat.

By doing these, we can become experts in our field or at the very least develop enough career capital to get us closer to finding our unique calling.

Very few people are living to their full potential. Even fewer are in touch with their inner core being, unique calling, or dharma (sacred duty). The path of most successful individuals (other than professional athletes) is usually not a straight line, but more of a connect-the-dots picture. We never know when a side road will lead us closer to our dharma. Therefore, it's critical to put ourselves in a position to be offered the opportunity to pursue other paths. This opportunity will only come to those few people who have been able to differentiate themselves in their work and who have the courage to move beyond their safe comfort zones. We must learn to treat everything that we do as the most important thing in the world and then do it with our very best effort. By constantly improving ourselves and delivering exceptional results, unexpected doors will open, and new paths will become visible.

Having new paths to consider is not sufficient to ensure success. In order to correctly navigate these roads of new opportunities, we need to be aware of what it is that makes us tick. What do we do at work that doesn't feel like work? When do we feel truly alive in our life? What did we love to do as a child before the indoctrination of school, society, and parents? By answering these and other questions, we can develop stretch goals for ourselves and then work hard each day to get them done. This rare self-awareness and exceptional effort can allow us to return to our core (the essence of our being) and move us closer to our unique version of great and meaningful work—the type of work that we are all meant to do.

CHAPTER 4

Hedonic Adaptation: The Most Important Principle You Never Learned!

I worked really hard to get to where I am but thought that I would be happier. I have a nice house, good job, healthy family, and overall, a very comfortable life—so why do I take it all for granted?

You'll become used to all of the positive things in your life. You'll take for granted your job, bigger house, new car, and even your family. Some call this human nature, while others use more scientific terms like hedonic adaptation. Simply stated, hedonic adaptation states that we will adapt to positive and negative stimuli that are constant. The Stoics believed that it was precisely because of this adaptation process that we should be indifferent to external conditions and events as they relate to our happiness. The new house, higher salary, or fancy sports car all produce temporary spikes in happiness (pleasure), but we quickly become used to these things and return to our baseline level of happiness. This is an amazing and critical principle to understand and, more importantly, to teach our kids.

Everyone should be able to recognize the adaptation process at work. When I asked my son whether the new MLB PlayStation game is worth the price, given that he has last year's game at home, he replies with an emphatic "Yes!" After a month, I repeated the same question, and his reply was a more tepid "maybe."

He has adapted. What is crucial in this situation is to have him understand his adaptation and remember it prior to future must-have purchases. Unfortunately, our consumer-driven society is based upon promoting the myth that accumulating bigger and better stuff is the path to happiness. It's our job as parents to dispel this myth and provide strategies and alternative paths for our children to become happier. It's our job as adults to discuss this principle with others and understand the futility in material accumulation as a means toward the Good Life.

The science behind hedonic adaptation is robust, and modern positive psychology continues to confirm what the Stoics believed two thousand years ago. From an evolutionary perspective, hedonic adaptation provides an advantage. If our emotional reactions did not decrease over time, we would not be able to differentiate more significant stimuli (new and important events) from less significant stimuli (old events that should fade into the background). If unable to adapt to new stimuli, we would become overwhelmed with emotion and unable to change or survive. The extent to which we adapt to negative versus positive events in our lives, however, does not appear to be equal. The research on hedonic adaptation to negative events is best described in a nineteen-year longitudinal prospective study by Richard E. Lucas (2007). Lucas followed German residents who experienced a government certified disability during the course of the study. This group of disabled residents experienced a significant and sustained drop in well-being after the onset of the disability compared with their predisability levels, even after income and employment status were controlled. Other studies evaluating hedonic adaptation to negative events support the findings from Lucas's investigation: the well-being levels of people who experienced significant negative life events (disability, unemployment, widowhood, or divorce) did show improvement over time but never fully recovered. In other words, they were not able to completely adapt to the event. This has serious implications in our happiness as we all need to be able to effectively cope with the inevitable struggles in life.

Unlike negative stimuli, we adapt rapidly to positive events in our lives. In a 1978 study of lottery winners, Brickman et al. (1978) showed that the winners were back to their baseline level of happiness within eighteen months after their big win. In a study by Lane (2000), there was no change in well-being over a fifty-year period when income tripled from 1940 to 1990. In a prospective study by Lucas and Clark (2006), German residents who married over the fifteen-year period of the study showed a significant boost in their happiness levels initially after the wedding but returned to their baseline levels after an average of two years. Finally, a second longitudinal study (Boswell et al. 2005) found that high-level managers who changed jobs over the course of the study also demonstrated boosts in their satisfaction after the move (a honeymoon effect similar to the marriage study), but their satisfaction plummeted within a year (hangover effect). This hangover effect is actually evidence of adaptation; this rapid adaptation to positive life events is a problem if our ultimate goal is to be happier. Sonia Lyubomirsky states in her terrific book *The How of Happiness* that "the quick and complete hedonic adaptation to positive events and to improvements in life circumstances is one of the greatest obstacles in raising and sustaining happiness."

A FORMULA FOR HAPPINESS: CHOOSE YOUR OPTIMAL RESPONSE

If we adapt slowly and incompletely to negative, often traumatic, events and very quickly and completely become used to the positive aspects that make us feel good (at least initially), how can we possibly sustain and improve our well-being? The answer lies in the formula for happiness outlined by Sheldon and Lyubomirsky (2004):

> H (happiness) = S (set point) 50 percent + C (external condition) 10 percent + V (volition or voluntary activities) 40 percent

Several behavioral genetic studies have shown that approximately 50 percent of the variability between people's happiness levels can be accounted for by genes. This genetic set point for most of us is a major impediment to raising levels of well-being and has led many researchers to conclude that happiness cannot be significantly changed. This formula also suggests that external conditions, for most people not afflicted by extreme poverty or trauma, play a relatively minor role in our happiness levels. The Stoics would agree. In fact, Epictetus would change this formula to read H= S + V as he (and other Stoic philosophers) did not believe any external condition or event should impact one's tranquility. This is an important conclusion that is supported by the research on hedonic adaptation to positive life events. We adapt to every good thing in our lives. Therefore, if we want to sustain and increase our well-being, we must forget about our genes, status, or wealth and focus on the voluntary activities, thoughts, and behaviors that provide up to 40 percent of our happiness levels. It's not where we live or what we accumulate that matters; it's what we do that makes all the difference.

If our intentional activities provide positive emotions and play a significant role in our well-being, won't we simply adapt to them as we would to a new car or bigger house? The answer is yes. We have all taken for granted our health as we wake up each day and are able to easily get out of bed. We have adapted to the presence of our spouse and family in our daily lives. We complain about our jobs and rarely consider the thrill of initially landing the position.

If an individual adapts to all things positive, then no matter what thrilling, meaningful, and wonderful experiences await her, these experiences will not make her any happier but instead may drive her to acquire even more new and thrilling things and risk placing herself squarely on a futile and desperate hedonic treadmill. (Brickman and Campbell, 1971).

Does this sound familiar? I know many people (including myself a few years ago) who fit this description. The good news for all of us is that people appear to vary in their rates of hedonic adaptation to both positive and negative events. More importantly, a significant number of individuals actually become happier over time. A twenty-two-year study of two thousand healthy veterans found that life satisfaction increased over these men's lives, peaked around age sixty-five, and did not start declining significantly until age seventy-five (Mroczek and Spiro, 2005). In the fifteen-year longitudinal study by Lucas (2007) of marital transitions, although most returned to their baseline levels of happiness, some individuals got happier and stayed happier after marriage. Additionally, while some widows' happiness plummeted and never fully recovered after their spouse's death, others actually became happier after the initial grieving period.

Given everyone's unique life circumstances, there are likely several reasons why some people appear to be more resilient to the adaptation process. According to Lyubomirsky, "The chief reason for this resilience is that people have the capacity to control the speed and extent of adaptation via intentional, effortful activities." The goal, based on Lyubomirsky's research, is for us to engage in activities and behaviors that will accelerate the adaptation process to negative events and slow down the process to positive events. This is not a trivial goal, given that over half of US adults will experience one severely traumatic event during their lives (Ozer and Weiss, 2004) and practically everyone, at some point, will experience moderate daily stress. Without the ability to cope (accelerate the hedonic adaptation process), many people will stay anxious, depressed, and frustrated as they struggle to move beyond the negative event. Figuring out which behaviors and activities will accelerate adaptation to negative stimuli depends upon our understanding of which intentional efforts are effective in slowing down the hedonic adaptation process to positive events.

My experience is what I agree to attend to. (William James)

One of the most useful ways that we can slow down or stop becoming used to all of the good things in our lives is to simply pay attention to them. What most people choose to focus on determines their experience and, in fact, becomes their life. As we think about our own lives, once a person, material possession, an activity, or job no longer grabs our attention, we have adapted to it. Conversely, anything or anyone that we are continually aware of or that keeps popping into our minds will be less prone to hedonic adaptation.

A study of owners of luxury cars showed that these drivers were no happier driving their expensive luxury automobiles during car trips than owners of small, two-door coupes unless they were thinking of their car's attributes while driving. (Schwarts, Kahneman, and Xu). If they were noticing the comfortable seats, terrific handling, or nice stereo system while driving, they reported higher levels of happiness compared with owners of nonluxury cars. Just as they were appreciating the good aspects of their cars, we can appreciate the good things in our lives. Tal Ben-Shahar states that "when we appreciate the good, the good appreciates." Lyubomirsky and Sheldon (2011) note that "people who continue to be aware of a positive activity change in their lives are less likely to adapt to it." The act of appreciation or paying attention to the good in our lives is one that can be intentionally chosen and habituated. If maintaining the correct level of attention is the antidote for hedonic adaptation, what is the best way to inoculate ourselves? More importantly, how do we make this into a habit? The answer lies in two key happiness interventions: gratitude and optimal frequency of activities.

GRATITUDE: THE QUICKEST PATH TO HAPPINESS

Many ancient religious and philosophical texts regard gratitude as one of the greatest virtues. Like any virtue, it must be deliberately practiced. We have all been told at some point in our lives to count our blessings and to give thanks for what we have. This common wisdom has been passed down for many generations. Most of us believe in this virtue of gratefulness as a component of happiness without needing evidence-based research studies. Recently, science has caught up with what ancient wisdom has been preaching for many years. Modern science, through the rapidly growing field of positive psychology, has eluci-dated clear benefits of cultivating gratitude on improved psychological, social, and physical well-being (Emmons 2003, Wood, Froh, and Geraghty 2010). In the original landmark study by Robert Emmons, considered to be the leading researcher on gratitude, participants were ran-domly assigned to one of three experimental conditions:

- Hassles
- Gratitude listing
- Either neutral life events or social comparison

Daily or weekly records were kept of their moods, coping and health behaviors, physical symptoms, and overall life satisfaction. The cultivation of a grateful affect through daily or weekly journaling "resulted in improved well-being, reduced physical complaints, increased exercise time, and overall more positive outlook compared with the groups detailing hassles or neutral life events" (Emmons 2003). There are many reasons for the causal benefit of gratitude on well-being: better coping skills to negative life events, reduced social comparisons, less materialistic pursuits, improved self-esteem, and pro-social moral behavior (Emmons 2010). As I began to research the mechanism and principles behind hedonic adaptation, it became clear to me that gratefulness works precisely because it's an effective antidote to the adaptation process.

A daily or weekly practice of expressing gratitude, either verbally or through journaling, forces us to pay attention to all of the good in our lives. This sense of paying attention or of active appreciation allows us to remember what we have, and by remembering, we are less prone to take the positive aspects of our lives for granted.

We now know through evidence-based research that developing and sustaining a grateful attitude is critical to optimal mental and physical health. Other studies elucidate the effect of gratitude on increased parasympathetic activity with resultant lower blood pressure and cortisol levels (McCraty and Childre, 2004). This has tremendous implications in our fight to effectively handle stress, lower the incidence of cardiovascular events, and ultimately live a more optimal life.

We know that gratitude is good for us and may be the most effective strategy for thwarting hedonic adaptation. How do we incorporate the practice of gratefulness into our busy lives? How do we teach ourselves, our children, and our peers to be more grateful? The regular practice of journaling has been heavily researched and found to be one of the most effective gratitude interventions available. As we discussed with the Stoics, both Seneca and Marcus Aurelius had a daily practice of journaling. The opening chapter of Marcus Aurelius's *Meditations* details his giving of thanks to people in his life. Interestingly, there has been recent evidence that, similar to the Stoic's practice of negative visualization, mentally subtracting the good from our lives may be more powerful in improving well-being than simply being thankful (Koo and Algoe 2008). For me, the practice of keeping a gratitude journal has been transformative. I have experimented with different methods and times of day to record my gratitude list. I have also tried various different frequencies ranging from daily to biweekly. The best method for me is to record a list of five things for which I am grateful. I do this in the early morning, usually before breakfast, and approximately three times per week. Not surprisingly, more frequent daily gratitude journaling became somewhat rote and lost its significance. I had adapted to the daily journaling practice. I can keep the practice fresh, engage in vivid visualization, and more effectively count my blessings when I journal three or four times per week. As I have been doing this practice for several years, I now find myself thinking of things throughout the day that I can write about in my gratitude journal. In essence, I'm more mindful of the things around me, more appreciative of the good and less affected by daily trivial annoyances. I'm not claiming to be a saint or to be free of worry and stress. I still become angry with my kids or upset at a difficult work situation. Those events will never completely be eliminated as long as we are active participants in our lives. But since I started journaling, the periods of feeling down have become shorter and are interspersed with longer periods of life satisfaction, thankfulness, and meaning that have become the norm for me.

VARIETY REALLY IS THE SPICE OF LIFE

Quantity affects quality. I love the simplicity and power of those three words. We know that hedonic adaptation to all of the good things in our lives is the greatest obstacle to improved happiness and that active appreciation of these things is an effective antidote. In addition to cultivating habits of gratefulness, another powerful way to maintain attention on the pleasant aspects of our lives is to vary their timing. By simply changing the frequency and intensity of certain pleasurable activities, we can slow down or halt our adaptation to them.

The optimal timing of positive and pleasurable activities is a constant battle for all of us. How do we know when there is too much of a good thing? At what point are we watching too much TV or having too much to drink? Is every day too much? How about exercise? Is there a point where training becomes excessive and ceases to provide the desired benefit? Aristotle defined virtue as the perfect mean between extremes, exemplifying the concept of moderation in all of our actions. This ability to moderate behavior and activities is critical in our fight against hedonic adaptation.

In addition to varying the frequency of positive actions,

we must also find ways to introduce variety into the action itself. Perhaps the most important area of our lives in which hedonic adaptation is so pervasive is with our spouses and intimate relationships. Without understanding the concept of hedonic adaptation, many people simply fall out of love with or grow bored with their partner. They search for new mates (to whom they have not yet adapted) in an effort to rekindle the sparks and excitement that they feel must be present at all times. Unfortunately, the cycle repeats itself as they grow more dissatisfied with their new relationship. As a first crucial step, we must recognize the presence of the adaptation process in our marriages.

One of the best ways to do this is by introducing variety through new experiences and goals that are shared with one another. Most couples stagnate: they eat at the same restaurants, they vacation at the same places, they have the same conversations, and generally have a worse relationship as time goes on. They simply stop growing. They stop learning. They stop experimenting. They stop living. The ability to evolve as a person and as a couple takes effort. It takes time. It requires prioritization, experimentation, and dedication.

We adapt quickly to the good in our lives, but by choosing intentional thoughts and activities, we can increase our levels of well-being. In order to sustain this boost of happiness, we must vary the intensity and timing of these pleasurable behaviors while expressing heartfelt gratitude for the good aspects of our lives. By doing this, we are able to continue to pay attention to all of the good around us. This active appreciation allows us to slow or halt the adaptation process, experience more joy, and ultimately become happier.

CHAPTER 5

MINDFULNESS—DON'T MISS LIFE TWICE!

Question: My life is passing by so quickly—why do I feel as if I am missing most of it?

Answer: Mindfulness, meditation, and time.

There is nothing the busy man is less busied with than living: there is nothing that is harder to learn...It takes the whole of life to learn how to live, and—what will perhaps make you ponder more—it takes the whole of life to learn how to die.

—SENECA, *ON THE SHORTNESS OF LIFE*

Most of us live with a constant stream of thoughts, worries, and to-do lists swirling around in our heads. We need more presence, more peace, and more purpose, but we find ourselves thinking about work while playing with our kids, surfing the internet while having a conversation with our spouse, or checking our phone at the first sign of solitude. It's estimated that we spend less than 20 percent of our lives truly engaged in what we are doing at any given moment. Being truly present is a rarity. Imagine how we could extend our actual lives if we could increase our presence from 20 percent to 50 percent of the time. That would add twenty-five to thirty years of real living to our lives. How can we figure out how to really be where we are, really do what we are doing, and really feel what we are feeling?

The weekend that my oldest son played his final basketball game at his school (kindergarten to eighth grade) was an emotional one for me. They had a special recognition ceremony for all of the eighth-grade players. The players walked with their parents while their favorite basketball memories, athletic achievements, and plans for high school were announced over the loudspeaker. The team went on to win a close game (35–33), but the real impact of the night, for me, was a reminder that life is short. I felt very sad when I thought of him heading to high school the following year and had already become nostalgic for his youth. He was only thirteen!

Why does this happen? Why can we not accept the imper-manence of things or accept that everything is always changing—minute by minute, day by day, year by year? Is that so hard? Mary Oliver, the famous poet, stated in a podcast (*On Being*, with Krista Tippet) that she finds comfort in the fact that everything just continues in one form or another—there is no beginning or end in nature. This is also a common belief in Hinduism and is a key tenet in the Bhagavad Gita. Intellectually, I understand the power of this belief, but emotionally, I feel different. I don't want us to lose our youth, our kids' childhoods, or our parents. It doesn't matter to me that things may evolve or continue in other forms once they are gone. I want these forms and everything that exists today to stay exactly as it is!

I know that I'm being unrealistic. This seems to be the problem with most of us. We want control over everything that happens. We want people to like us. We want our kids to make the team. We want our bosses to pay us more money. We want to get into better shape. We want to be happier. Unfortunately, we forget that we don't have any control over the ultimate outcome—our death and the dying that we do every day. We all seem to be afraid of dying, but most of us act as though we will live forever. We spend our time wasting most of our time. We get angry at minor inconveniences and fail to appreciate how good we really have it. We look ahead to the weekend or our next vacation and simply go through the motions at work. We expect people to act in a certain way and become upset when they act differently. We gossip, drink, and watch TV in an effort to relax. I'm guilty of all of this! This is no way to live, however, and we can do better. Rather than fill our lives with distractions to avoid thinking about our mortality, we must come to grips with death in order to learn how to live.

We all face the same pain. We face the pain of attachment to things as they are. We face the pain of longing for a certain future that may never come. We face the pain of existing, but not really living. We face the pain of missing life twice—once as it happens and another as we look back. We face the pain of not making a difference. We face the pain of not knowing why we often feel like crying. We face the pain of remembering our youth. We face the pain of looking in the mirror. We face the pain inside of our heads.

These feelings have been present for thousands of years. How can we live in the present while learning to live well in the future? How do we make the most of today while ensuring a better tomorrow? How can we stop worrying over things that we know won't matter in a month or a year? These are important questions to answer or at least ponder. Buddhism states that everything is always changing. It could be overt changes like getting older or the passing of seasons or even subtler forms of change, like our different perceptions from moment to moment.

This concept of impermanence threatens our sense of mortality. As we try to exist in the world, we tend to filter the ever-changing nature of the universe into what we think is a more controllable and permanent reality. We conceptualize instead of directly experiencing our environment because we fear impermanence—it signals our own mortality and our own lack of control of our ultimate existence. This fear creates the filter; in doing so, it suppresses true awakening, true experience, and true living.

Life is short, but the shortness of life should not be an excuse to hurry up and produce. It's just the opposite. We must slow down and savor the moments. What matters is our ability to make the most of things while they exist. Really feel, appreciate, and love them. That is the key to impermanence and our lack of control—being present in an ever-changing moment. Of course we can do what we can to ensure an optimal future. We can take care of our health, make smart financial decisions, and spend our days (so precious and few that they are) in the right way—filled with intention, purpose, and presence—so that we may one day look back on a life well lived.

Looking back to that final game, I knew as it was happening that one day I was going to miss that day. As a result, I really enjoyed having both sets of grandparents there to watch my son play that night. I felt grateful that all of us were together at dinner celebrating life rather than mourning the passage of time. I looked on with pride as my son smiled and conversed with his classmates. These are the ways to live. To realize that life is really short and to accept that things are constantly changing. To try to live each day as if it were our last. To really feel and appreciate each moment. Only by living this way can we really live. Time may be slipping away, my breaths may be dwindling in number, but my next breath is deep and divine. The past is gone, and the future may never come (certainly in the way we expect). What we have now is all we have. Smile, breathe, feel, appreciate—repeat.

WHY MEDITATE?

Imagine a pill that is proven to reduce the risk of heart attacks, stroke, and death by 49 percent; significantly reduce blood pressure, rates of anxiety, depression, and substance abuse; statistically improve academic performance, creativity, and the length and quality of life. Additionally, this pill has no side effects, is available to anyone at any time, and is free of charge. Fortunately for us, this pill does exist. This wonder drug is called Transcendental Meditation (TM). TM was founded by Maharishi Mahesh Yogi, who developed the practice to be independent of a belief in Hinduism or any other religion. There are over 350 peer-reviewed publications investigating the effectiveness of TM on reducing stress-related disorders, improving cognitive function, lowering risk of cardiovascular events, and leading a higher quality of life. The research behind TM is so robust that the American Heart Association issued a scientific statement specifically endorsing TM as "the only meditation technique that has been shown to lower blood pressure and that this reduction in blood pressure has been associated with substantially reduced rates of death, heart attack, and stroke" (Brook et al.). The scientific statement goes on to state that as an additional advantage, TM may provide a wide range of health and psychological benefits beyond blood pressure and cardiovascular risk reduction.

Given all of the documented benefits, why aren't all physicians practicing and recommending TM? If TM were in a pill form, it would create a billion-dollar industry with pharmaceutical sales reps visiting every physician practice. In our world of instant gratification with minimal effort, practicing TM takes more work than swallowing a pill. Moreover, meditation still has a religious connotation as a practice rooted in Eastern traditions of Buddhism and Hinduism. Even with these challenges, TM is practiced by millions of people worldwide, including many famous celebrities such as Howard Stern, Ellen DeGeneres, and David Lynch.

As I struggled to balance competing roles as a father of four children, husband, son, brother, and physician executive, I have known that meditation would probably be good for me. I have tried to meditate off and on for many years with little success. I have attempted different techniques of mindful focus on my body and breath, but I've struggled to achieve the desired state of stillness or quiet in my mind. All of that changed with TM. The use of a mantra for me was the key to finding the calm I was after. Rather than focus or concentrate on breath or a part of the body, simply returning to and repeating the mantra allows me to go deeper into a relaxed state. I cannot over-emphasize how much my TM practice has helped me at work. In an environment with constant demands on my time and difficult interactions with others, I have found that TM makes me less aggressive, more empathetic, less stressed, and generally better able to live each day according to my best self. This is not without effort. My morning meditation usually takes place in my car before I head upstairs to my office. I enter the office feeling (knowing) that one of the most important tasks of my day is already complete. On the weekends, I'll often meditate in my car at sporting events for my children. During many trips to baseball tournaments out of town, I welcome the early arrival time for warm-ups as an opportunity to meditate. This is especially useful for the anxiety that I, along with most parents, feel during sporting events. We all want our kids to perform well.

One idea that has been helpful for me is to let go of any expectations or results when I meditate. During some sessions, I'll enter such a peaceful stillness with little effort and other times will struggle to keep returning to the mantra. Both types of experiences are useful. I can't predict whether the restless session may, in fact, be more beneficial precisely because my mind appears to be so unsettled at that time. The key with meditation, like any other rewarding endeavor, is deliberate practice. Meditating consistently, even when you have other things that you could be doing, is critical.

Meditating is a unique and rewarding experience. It's the feeling of refueling myself similar to the filling up of a gas tank in a car. I feel a rush of solitude float throughout my body as tension is replaced by calm. I lose tactical sensation of my hands and feet. I'm floating above my body as it's being recharged completely. I believe with all of my heart that our schools, workplaces, societies, and world would be greatly improved if everyone started their day with meditation. A significant amount of research on the benefits of meditation in schools is currently being conducted and the projected results are astounding. Improved academic performance, reduced behavioral problems, increased resilience, and lower anxiety and stress have all been associated with meditation programs worldwide. Of course some of these are called "quiet time" or something other than meditation to ensure the secular nature of the practice. Regardless of the name of the program, teaching kids to be able to go inward to find a place of calmness and acceptance rather than looking externally to friends, alcohol, or drugs is a tremendous achievement.

There are many useful websites, classes, and books on how to meditate. TM has worked well for me, but I know several other people who practice mindful meditation or loving-kindness meditation with great success. In a world filled with constant stimuli, effective and efficient methods of relaxation are difficult to find. Being able to bathe one's mind in stillness each day may be one of the greatest returns on investment ever known to man. Whatever form ultimately works for you, I urge you to begin experimenting today. It's well worth the effort to become addicted to this wonder drug!

EFFECTIVE USE OF TIME AND STRENGTHS: THE 80/20 RULE AND THE WAY OF THE ESSENTIALIST

It is not a daily increase, but a daily decrease. Hack away at the inessentials.

—BRUCE LEE

I do believe in simplicity. It is astonishing as well as sad, how many trivial affairs even the wisest thinks he must attend to in a day thinking about time as a dwindling, nonrenewable resource to be hoarded.

—HENRY DAVID THOREAU

What if you learned that only few of the activities that you do are responsible for most of your happiness? What if someone told you that performing a couple of key tasks at work will cause most of your success? What if you realized that spending time with just a handful of people provides the greatest amount of happiness? To put it another, more depressing way, what if most of the things you do provide the least amount of success, pleasure, and satisfaction? What if most of the people with whom you spend the majority of time provide you with only a small amount of happiness? This is the 80/20 rule, sometimes called Pareto's principle. It's named after an Italian economist, Vilfredo Pareto, who studied the distribution of wealth among landowners and found that 80 percent of the land was owned by 20 percent of landowners. Simply put, it states that 80 percent of results flow from 20 percent of causes. For example, we wear 20 percent of our clothes 80 percent of the time. We send 80 percent of emails to 20 percent of our contacts. We spend 80 percent of our time with people giving us 20 percent of our happiness. In business, 20 percent of customers provide 80 percent of the profits. Twenty percent of your growth initiatives will result in 80 percent of extra future value. Only 20 percent of high performers are responsible for 80 percent of the organization's success. This is a powerful rule and is described in great detail in Richard Koch's book *The 80/20 Principle*.

The 80/20 principle describes an imbalance between input

and output. To put it another way, there are some inputs (thoughts, actions, goals) that can drive much greater outputs (money, success, happiness). Understanding and exploiting this inequity is the key to optimizing and directing effort toward desired outcomes. Life is better lived if we can maximize the return on our most precious investment (time) for the things that really matter. This is where the movement of essentialism is really useful. This concept or way of life is skillfully articulated by Greg McKeown in his book *Essentialism: The Disciplined Pursuit of Less*. Essentialism is (essentially) the 80/20 rule on steroids. Where the 80/20 rule states that a minority of activities provide the majority of benefit, essentialism states that we should actively eliminate everything that is not important and focus only on those few areas that are vital. Essentialism is not a time management system designed to get more things done—it's a way of life to get the right things done. Essentialism is about doing less but better. It implores us to ask ourselves what is truly essential and to eliminate everything else. It's about having the self-awareness to focus only on the things that truly make a difference—for our work, for our family, and for our soul.

Living the way of the essentialist is also about having the courage and discipline to cut out the noise in our lives. We live in a world with an almost constant barrage of information, opportunities, and other mind-numbing stimuli. It's easy to become overwhelmed and float through life, allowing others and society to define how to spend your life. I mean "spend" in the literal sense because once we have made a withdrawal in the currency of time, we cannot replenish that bank account. We need to proactively invest our resources to figure out what values we hold dear, what exactly we want to be doing with our limited time on earth, and what provides us with meaning and happiness. Once we have figured out our essentials, we have to relentlessly and ruthlessly protect them and eliminate everything else. By embracing essentialism, we can distinguish between the trivial many from the vital few, eliminate the nonessentials, and remove any obstacles that stand in our way on the path toward the Good Life.

Reading, journaling, and meditating have really helped me to figure out what few activities and pursuits are most meaningful to me. Writing this book has become one of my essentials. Raising a close-knit family unit filled with love, optimism, gratitude, and service is another nonnegotiable pursuit. Continuing to evolve as individuals and as a couple for Tricia and myself is vital. Spending more time having real conversations with people I care about is crucial. Having complete congruence between what I think, say, and do (the definition of integrity) has become a clear focus for me. Staying mentally and physically fit through nutrition, yoga, meditation, and sports is a top priority. Contributing to the success and well-being of others is one of my daily goals. By clearly defining all of my true essentials, I can easily (or at least confidently) say no to the many nonessential requests for my time. I can choose to go to yoga over my lunch hour rather than eat at my desk while mindlessly surfing the internet. I can choose to write rather than going golfing for four hours. I can choose to play with the kids rather than checking email for the hundredth time that day. I can choose to block some time each week in my schedule to meet with two of my best friends. I can choose to understand and optimize the few key drivers for success in my business rather than attend meetings with little yield.

By doing the hard work of identifying your vital few, you can distinguish and eliminate the trivial many. Constantly ask yourself, "What is the most important thing I could be doing right now?" and go do it. Life is too short to waste on things that don't matter. I'll end this discussion with two quotes that really bring this point home:

> Most of what exists in the universe—our actions, and all other forces, resources, and ideas—has little value and yields little result; on the other hand, a few things work fantastically well and have tremendous impact. (Richard Koch)

> You cannot overestimate the unimportance of practically everything. (John Maxwell)

Conclusion

THE FUTURE: POSITIVE PHILOSOPHY AS THE ROADMAP TO FLOURISHING

This book combines the goals of philosophy with the practical, evidence-based tools of modern positive psychology into a single unified system: Positive Philosophy.

Positive Philosophy encompasses important core principles of philosophy and ancient wisdom:

1. A focus on human flourishing as the ultimate goal in life.
2. The use of reason and self-regulation to act with virtue.
3. The concept of personal duty or unique human potential (dharma) and the need to fulfill this duty with

deliberate practice while relinquishing the fruits of our labor.

4. The feeling of being present in an ever-changing moment.
5. Interconnectedness to others along with the universe as a whole.

Positive Philosophy also utilizes the key tenets of positive psychology:

1. The cultivation of an attitude of gratitude and optimism.
2. A focus on using one's unique strengths to fully realize potential.
3. The concept of service to others as a path toward the Meaningful Life.
4. The importance of adversity and grit in long-term success and well-being.
5. The futility of material possessions as a means to happiness (hedonic adaptation).

I believe that Positive Philosophy can bring a sense of tranquility, meaning, and joy to our lives. By combining the original goals of philosophy with the practical, scientifically validated tools of positive psychology, Positive Philosophy allows us to understand what it means to live a good life and, more importantly, to be able to effectively translate this knowledge into actually living one.

I can remember a time with significant changes occurring at work. I was mulling over protecting radiologist salaries in the face of declining reimbursements, increased service level expectations, and an overall very different radiology marketplace. As I was getting in my car one morning, I realized that these are the moments that we need Positive Philosophy the most. It's exactly during these times of change, struggle, anxiety, and uncertainty that a practical code of living—one that preaches a focus on what I can control, acceptance of impermanence, appreciation of what is going well, optimistic approach to new experiences, and most of all choosing an optimal response—is crucial. Positive Philosophy cannot be esoteric principles written in the abstract. It needs to stand the rigor of daily life and daily struggles. It needs to solve problems, teach us how to act, return us to equanimity, and most of all keep us on the path to a good life. We must stand arm in arm with Positive Philosophy as we learn how to live lives of substance and meaning. These types of lives are never easy, not very comfortable at times, and certainly not common. If I believe that adversity is underrated and critical to periods of explosive growth and creativity, then Positive Philosophy (as a practical code of living) can serve as a type of full body armor to help us move forward on the battlefield of life.

While self-help books, blogs, and coaches offer great tips and insight on destructive behaviors and situations that can impede our happiness, most of the advice is centered on alleviating the symptoms while ignoring the disease. The root of the illness is a fundamental gap that exists between how we could be living and how we are actually living. It's a gap between our true potential and our current level of output. It's a gap between being completely engaged in our lives and simply going through the motions. It's a gap between responding as our best self and reacting in our typical way. This gap or shortfall in our potential, our presence, and our actions is the true illness. It's the real source of discontent in most of our lives. In order to close these gaps, we need a personal operating system for optimal living that combines the timeless truths of ancient wisdom with modern, evidence-based science. We need Positive Philosophy.

The largest and most important gap that most of us face is a gap in our potential. We often operate at a potential deficit. There is a gap between our current output and our deep unrealized ability. This shortfall leads to anxiety and tension as we all crave impact, meaning, and purpose. We have two choices to deal with this tension. The most common path is to strive toward a tensionless state. We fill our lives up with TV, alcohol, and other distractions in an attempt to discharge this tension. We focus on the trivial and mundane at the expense of the valuable and essential. We consume our self-worth through status and popularity of ourselves and our kids.

The problem with this approach is that a state devoid of any tension or struggle also lacks meaning and purpose, which are critical to the Good Life. We cannot overcome our deep discontent simply by making things easier or seeking pleasure as our ultimate goal in life. Our discontent continues, which creates a larger gap to our full potential. This leads to progressively increased tension as we get older. Unless we break this vicious cycle of unfulfilled potential leading to discontent and release of tension which ultimately leads to more discontent, we will never find tranquility and a state of flourishing. The more difficult, but correct path to follow, is to recognize that our discontent lies within us—not in our friends, spouse, environment, kids, or bank account. The true source of anxiety and unrest for many of us is a deep (often subconscious) understanding that we are not living to our full ability. We know that we are not fully alive but often are just going through the motions. The real problem that we face is this: until we unlock our full potential, we will never be able to truly flourish. As we have learned from the teachings of Aristotle, the Bhagavad Gita, and the Stoics, achieving a state of human flourishing or eudaimonia is the key to a life well lived. This is the reason that this gap in our potential is so damaging—it prevents us from flourishing. As this is the subject of lifelong study, it's important that we all become students of life and for life. It's the most important subject that we will study.

The exact path to fully realize our potential will vary, but there are several common steps. The first step is the need to develop insight and awareness of our strengths, inclinations, and unique abilities. Several questions to ask include: What do we care about? What do we do that doesn't feel like work? What would we pay to do? What would we do if we knew we couldn't fail? In other words, we all need to find our dharma (sacred duty)—a clear vision of our fully realized potential in this world.

It's important to remember that this vision of our full potential may not be clear at first and will likely take many twists and turns over a lifetime. The key is to keep asking the right questions to help guide us toward what really matters. Once we have this focus, we need to put in the work. There are no shortcuts to living a life to your full potential. It requires deliberate practice and a laser focus on always doing your best. The 80/20 rule and essentialism are critical concepts that provide an effective framework for this type of focus and effort.

On the road to fully developing one's potential, we need to let go of the results. As preached by the Stoics and the Bhagavad Gita, we must focus on what we can control (our attitude, actions, and degree of effort), not on what is out of our control (outcomes, opinions of others, and other external indicators of success). Given that our actions and behaviors are within our control and therefore key to fully realizing our potential, we must learn how to act well in order to live well. Unfortunately, this is often easier said than done. Similar to the potential deficit, many of us also have an action deficit. This is a gap between how we normally act and how we should act.

It's much easier to act well if you have a firm vision of what that looks like. We all face mind-numbing stimuli and distractions every day. Instead of allowing our emotional reactions to guide our behavior to these daily struggles, we can utilize three simple concepts that will help us choose our optimal response. The Golden Rule has been well described in many different cultures, but the basic premise is the same: treat others as you would like to be treated. This is a very powerful mandate that can inspire us to act with humility, compassion, and tranquility. However, as with anything worthwhile, it takes practice—especially when someone upsets us or doesn't act according to our wishes. Another simple concept is having a clear understanding and practice of integrity. The best definition of integrity that I have read is having complete congruence between what we think, say, and do. There will be many opportunities to cheat, take shortcuts, bend the truth, or intentionally mislead others. If we can remember to live in harmony between our thoughts, words, and actions, the right choice or way to live becomes much clearer. It's usually black or white instead of many shades of gray. The final component of acting well is to have a detailed vision of our ideal or best self—a vision of our fully realized potential. This is an exercise that can be very powerful if we take the time to reflect and journal on how we would like to see ourselves acting each day. What essential areas of your life would you focus on? What are the key virtues that your best self embodies in your interactions with others? How does your ideal self handle stress and anxiety? By clearly formulating this vision of our best self, we can create a daily mantra or set of rules to live by. An example of mine is the following:

I am present.

I accept each moment as if I had chosen it.

I give each moment my undivided focus. This is it.

I focus on what is working well, what I can control—my breath, my words, and my actions.

I am grateful for the health, safety, and happiness of my family, which is the most important thing in my life.

I am playful.

I smile, laugh, play, and joke around each day.

I live with integrity.

There is harmony between what I think, say, and do in each moment.

I am a great listener.

I practice active listening every day, and I never criticize.

I am compassionate and generous with my knowledge, time, and money.

I work to make the people and world around me better than I found them.

I am optimistic and enthusiastic.

I realize that life is full of both joy and challenges. It is my response to the situation that determines my happiness.

I focus on the positive strengths in others and myself.

While I'll never get to the top of the mountain, I know that I'm climbing the right one. So let us act with integrity, according to our best self, and treat others as we want to be treated. In this way, we can act well so that we may also live well.

The final gap that must be closed is a deficit in our presence. This is the difference between being truly engaged in each moment and simply trying to get to the next activity. This remains an area of constant struggle for me and is without a doubt my largest deficit. My goal is to continue to improve slightly each year. The mindfulness movement is more popular than ever as many of us realize the extensive toll that unlimited access to email, social media, and activities has taken on our well-being. Rather than have conversations, we now text or email each other. Instead of playing with our kids, we drive them to private coaches and organized sporting events. While out with friends, we post pictures online to document our great time instead of actually having fun. We have traded substance for speed, effectiveness for efficiency, and living for existing.

The title of the great book by Jon Kabat-Zinn, *Wherever You Go, There You Are*, is a great mantra for reclaiming our presence. Repeating this many times during the day can help to bring you back to the present moment. Taking deep breaths particularly during times of increased stress or anxiety can help to activate the parasympathetic system. This system is the counterbalance to our usual fight-or-flight sympathetic response system that is, unfortunately, hyperactive for most of us. Meditation is probably the single most effective activity that we can practice to become more mindful. A steady practice of meditation can allow us to become less reactive, less stressed, and more present. Given the robust research behind the positive health benefits of meditation, we will, in the near future, consider meditation as a daily ritual similar to brushing our teeth or going for a run.

These three gaps in our potential, our actions, and our presence must be addressed if we are to truly flourish during our short time on this planet. Find out what you're meant to do—what only you can do—your sacred duty or place in the cosmic order. Unleash this potential by committing to it fully through deliberate practice. Be present in the process, act according to your best self, and let go of the results. Apply this fully realized potential for a purpose larger than yourself. Live virtuously in harmony with others and nature. Fight hedonic adaptation with gratitude, timing, and variety. Appreciate adversity and know that the effort, not results, leads to strength. These few principles enable all of us to lead lives filled with meaning, service, virtue, and impact. These are lives that feel good, lives that matter—the kind of life that we were all meant to live.

I had the opportunity to test these principles during a very emotional time. One of my best friends from high school lost his struggle with leukemia. I remember days hanging out in my room, listening to music—we were both huge REO Speedwagon fans—shooting nerf hoops, and talking about life. We were not sure of what life would bring, but we knew we were destined for big things. Denny was always more confident than I was, and I would listen to his advice closely. He seemed to have most things figured out. I was struggling with my own identity, caught between my Indian and American friends. I would often put up a façade to people in order to hide my deep insecurity. An insecurity about my name, my skin color, my parent's accents, etc. It was a tough time but, in retrospect, a much-needed experience. With Denny, my insecurities fell away. He knew me for all of my faults and still wanted to be friends.

I remember a game that we used to play while shooting hoops in my room. If I made this shot, then so-and-so would like me. If he made his shot, then the girl he wanted to ask to prom would say yes. We were in search of sure answers to a never-ending list of questions and concerns. We didn't realize it at the time, but we were sharing something very valuable yet so rare in our society (especially as we grow up)—vulnerability. Our questions were not filtered and carefully worded to hide our inner struggles—they were, in fact, our deepest fears, and we shared them boldly with each other.

About a year ago, I came across the following quote: "Be kind, for everyone is fighting a great battle." Everyone is, indeed, suffering in their own way. This suffering can come in many forms. It may be a life filled with distractions (TV, alcohol, gossip) that helps hide the pain of unrealized potential. It could be an excessive focus on our child's popularity, athletic performance, or academic achievement that helps to hide our own feelings of insecurity. It could be a real battle for your health that makes you realize what truly matters in life. Whatever the cause of the pain, we all suffer in some way. We are uncomfortable in the present but anxious for the future. We try to stabilize an ever-changing external environment while our internal world never finds peace. The problem of suffering is exacerbated by our unwillingness to discuss or even acknowledge it.

I still struggle with many things. How do we raise good kids who care about the world and not just their next video game? How do we find the balance between pushing our children to their full potential and letting them enjoy their childhood? How do we create a close-knit family in the midst of competing activities and distractions?

I used to suffer over questions like these. Was I on the path toward the Meaningful Life? What will I be remembered for when I'm gone? Would I reach my full potential? These were big questions that caused a large amount of anxiety and discontent, especially in the difficult time of a close friend's death. But by embracing the principles of Positive Philosophy that I have outlined in this book, I have been able to answer these questions and consequently lessen the amount of suffering that I felt, particularly in times of stress. Focusing on what was in my control—telling

Denny how much he meant to me, working on my unique potential, applying this potential to serve others, and acting with integrity as my best self in the process—gave me strength to both grieve and accept this unlucky card that Denny drew in life.

I'm grateful to have had a friend like Denny growing up and am even more thankful that we were able to reconnect before he passed away. We have all been blessed to have these types of friends. Someone who we shared our deepest secrets, our big dreams, and many laughs with while developing into the people we are today. These people touched our core and made life a little less lonely. We need to reach out to these friends and remember the power of real connection. The power of showing who we really are. The power of admitting we are afraid. The power of vulnerability.

NEXT STEPS

The principles outlined in this book are not complex. In fact, they are simple. They are simple but not easy. As with anything worthwhile, they require some planning, effort, and time. The rewards are tremendous and are an exponential return on the investment!

For those who, like me, appreciate the simplicity of daily checklists, this table provides a roadmap to an optimal life with a daily action plan.

FOCUS	TIME OF DAY	LENGTH OF TIME	DETAILS
Gratitude	Upon waking	1 minute	Write or visualize three things you're thankful for. Try to vary these and truly appreciate their presence in your life.
Negative Visualization	Anytime	1 minute	Imagine yourself without your job, spouse, children, health, parents, or whatever else is important to you. Pick one item and mentally subtract it from your life. Try to really imagine what it would be like if this aspect was gone.
Meditation		5 to 20 minutes	TM, loving-kindness meditation, or simply follow your breath.
Developing Potential	Daily	20 to 30 minutes	Identify a goal that aligns with your unique strengths and inner core.
Exercise	Daily	15 minutes	Any activity that gets your heart beating quickly.

It's important to note that you can spread out the steps throughout the day. I like to meditate and work on my potential in the morning, practice gratitude and negative visualization while driving, and exercise before dinner. This provides short bursts of meaningful activities throughout the day while allowing me to focus on work and family as well. It's up to you to experiment with what works best for your schedule.

You are the architect of your ideal life. Use the concepts and exercises in this book to begin to design it. It's not an overnight solution, and your life won't immediately change for the better. But by using these principles, you can develop your abilities to fully realize your unique potential in the service of something larger than yourself. That's where the Good Life is found. Enjoy the journey!

BIBLIOGRAPHY

Aristotle. *Nichomachean Ethics*. Translated by Terence Irwin. Indianapolis: Hackett Publishing Company, 1999.

Aurelius, Marcus. *Meditations*. New York: Dover Publications, 1997.

New American Standard Reader's Pew Bible. California: Foundation Publications, 1998.

Ben-Shahar, Tal. *Happier: Learn the Secrets to Daily Joy and Lasting Fulfillment*. New York: McGraw Hill, 2007.

Bhagavad Gita. Translated by Eknath Easwaran. Boston: Shambhala Library, 2004.

Boswell, W.R., J.T. Boudreau, and J. Tichy. "The relationship between employee job change and job satisfaction: the honeymoon-hangover effect." *Journal of Applied Psychology* 90, no. 5 (September 2005): 882–92.

Brickman, P., and D. T. Campbell. "Hedonic relativism and planning the good society." In *Adaptation-level Theory: A Symposium,* edited by M. H. Appley, 287–302. New York: Academic Press, 1972.

Brickman, P., D. Coates, and R. Janoff-Bulman. "Lottery Winners and Accident Victims: Is Happiness Relative?" *Journal of Personality and Social Psychology* 36 (1978): 917–927. doi: 10.1037/0022-3514.36.8.917.

Brook, R. D., et al. "Beyond Medications and Diet: Alternative Approaches to Lowering Blood Pressure: A Scientific Statement from the American Heart Association." *Hypertension* 61, no. 6 (June 2013):1360-83.

Collins, J., and J. Porras. *Built to Last*. New York: Harper Business, 1994.

Cope, Stephen. *The Great Work of Your Life: A Guide for the Journey to Your True Calling*. New York: Bantam Books, 2012.

Covey, Stephen R. *The 7 Habits of Highly Effective People: Restoring the Character Ethic*. New York: Free Press, 2004.

Dweck, Carol S. *Mindset: The New Psychology of Success*. New York: Random House, 2006.

Emmons, R. A., and M. E. McCullough. "Counting blessings versus burdens: Experimental studies of gratitude and subjective well-being in daily life." *Journal of Personality and Social Psychology* 84 (2003): 377-389.

Emmons, R. A., and M. E. McCullough. *The Psychology of Gratitude*. New York: Oxford University Press, 2004.

Epictetus. *Enchiridion*. 12th Media Services, 2018.

Ericsson, K. Anders. "The role of deliberate practice in the acquisition of expert performance." *Psychological Review* 100, no. 3 (1993): 363-406.

Eskreis-Winkler, L., A.L. Duckworth, E. Shulman, and S. Beal. "The grit effect: predicting retention in the military, the workplace, school and marriage." *Frontiers in Personality Science and Individual Differences* 5, no. 36 (2014): 1-12. PDF.

Franklin, Benjamin. *The Autobiography of Benjamin Franklin*. Dover Thrift Editions, 1996.

Frey, Bruno S., and Alois Stutzer. *Happiness and Economics*. New Jersey: Princeton University Press, 2001.

Gandhi, Mohandas Karamchand, and Mahatma Gandhi. *Autobiography: The Story of My Experiments with Truth*. Translated by Mahadev Desai. New York: Dover, 1983.

Garfield, Jay L. *The Meaning of Life: Perspectives from the World's Great Intellectual Traditions*. Chantilly, VA: Teaching Co., 2011.

Gospel of Thomas. Translated by Stevan Davies. Boston: Shambhala Library, 2004.

Greene, Robert. *Mastery*. New York: Viking, 2012.

Hendricks, Gay. *The Big Leap: Conquer Your Hidden Fear and Take Life to the Next Level*. New York: Harper Collins, 2009.

Hill, Patrick, and Nicholas Turiano. "Purpose in Life as a Predictor of Mortality across Adulthood." *Psychological Science* 25, no. 7 (May 2014): 1482-1486.

Irvine, William B. *A Guide to the Good Life: The Ancient Art of Stoic Joy*. New York: Oxford University Press, 2008.

Kabat-Zinn, Jon. *Wherever You Go, There You Are: Mindfulness Meditation in Everyday Life*. New York: Hyperion, 1994.

Koch, Richard. *The 80/20 Principle*. New York: Doubleday, 1998.

Koo, M., S.B. Algoe, T.D. Wilson, and D.T. Gilbert. "It's a wonderful life: mentally subtracting positive events improves people's affective states, contrary to their affective forecasts." *Journal of Personality and Social Psychology* 95, no. 5 (2008): 1217-1224.

Lane, R.E. "Diminishing Returns to Income, Companionship – and Happiness." *Journal of Happiness Studies* 1, no. 1 (March 2000): 103-119. https://doi.org/10.1023/A:1010080228107

Lucas, R.E. "Long-term disability is associated with lasting changes in subjective well-being: Evidence from two nationally representative longitudinal studies." *Journal of Personality and Social Psychology* 92, no. 4 (2007): 717.

Lucas, R.E., and M.B. Donnellan. "How stable is happiness? Using the STARTS model to estimate the stability of life satisfaction." *Journal of Research in Personality* 41, no. 5 (2007): 1091-1098.

Lucas, R. "Time Does Not Heal All Wounds: A Longitudinal Study of Reaction and Adaptation to Divorce." *Psychological Science* 16 (2005): 945-950.

Lucas, R. E., A. E. Clark, Y. Georgellis, and E. Diener. "Reexamining adaptation and the set point model of happiness: Reactions to changes in marital status." *Journal of Personality and Social Psychology* 84, no. 3 (2003): 527-539.

Lyubomirsky, Sonya. *The How of Happiness: A Scientific Approach to Getting the Life You Want*. New York: Penguin Press, 2008.

Lyubomirsky S., R. Dickerhoof, J.K. Boehm, and K.M. Sheldon. "Becoming happier takes both a will and a proper way: an experimental longitudinal intervention to boost well-being." *Emotion* 11, no. 2 (April 2011): 391-402. doi: 10.1037/a0022575.

Maslow, Abraham H. *Toward a Psychology of Being*. New York: J. Wiley & Sons, 1999.

McCraty, R., and D. Childre. "The grateful heart: The psychophysiology of appreciation." In *The Psychology of Gratitude*, edited by R. A. Emmons and M. E. McCullough, 230-255. New York, NY: Oxford University Press, 2004.

McCraty, Rollin, and Robert A. Rees. *The Central Role of the Heart in Generating and Sustaining Positive Emotions: Handbook of Positive Psychology*, 2nd edition. Oxford Library of Psychology, 2002 (50).

McKeown, Greg. *Essentialism: The Disciplined Pursuit of Less*. New York: Crown Business, 2014.

Mroczek, D. K., and A. Spiro. "Personality change influences mortality in older men." *Psychological Science*, 18, no. 5 (2007): 371-376.

Ozer, Emily J., and Daniel S. Weiss. "Who Develops Posttraumatic Stress Disorder?" *Current Directions in Psychological Science* 13, no. 4 (2004): 169-172.

Newport, Cal. *So Good They Can't Ignore You: Why Skills Trump Passion in the Quest for the Work You Love*. New York: Business Plus, 2012.

Schwarz, N., D. Kahneman, and J. Xu. "Global and episodic reports of hedonic experience." In *Using Calendar and Diary Methods in Life Events Research*, edited by R. Belli, D. Alwin and F. Stafford. Newbury Park, CA: Sage, in press.

Seneca, Lucius Annaeus. *Letters from a Stoic*. Translated by Robin Campbell. Harmondsworth: Penguin, 1969.

Seneca, Lucius Annaeus. *Moral Letters*. Translated by Robin Campbell. Harmondsworth: Penguin, 1969.

Seneca, Lucius Annaeus. *On the Shortness of Life*. Translated by C.D.N. Costa. New York: Penguin Books, 2005.

Sheldon K.M., S. Lyubomirsky. "Achieving sustainable new happiness: Prospects, practices, and prescriptions." In *Positive Psychology in Practice*, edited by A. Linley, S. Joseph, 127-145. Hoboken, NJ: John Wiley & Sons, 2004.

Stobeaus, John. In *Anthology* 2, 5b1-2 (II-95).

Tippet, Krista, and Mary Oliver. "Listening to the World." *On Being*. Podcast audio, October 15, 2015.

Tolle, Eckhart. *The Power of Now*. Vancouver: Namaste Publishing, 2004; and Novato, CA: New World Library, 1999.

Wood, A.M., J.J. Froh, and A.W. Geraghty. "Gratitude and well-being: a review and theoretical integration." *Clinical Psychology Review* 30, no. 7 (November 2010): 890-905.

About the Author

 **SANJ KATYAL** holds a bachelor of science with university honors in chemical and biomedical engineering from Carnegie Mellon University and a medical degree from New York University School of Medicine.

Sanj also holds certifications in positive psychology and positive psychology coaching from the Wholebeing Institute. He has published and lectured extensively on well-being and the science of happiness to audiences ranging from college students to physicians. He is currently investigating the effectiveness of positive psychology interventions on physician wellness and burnout.

His hobbies include kayaking, writing, and traveling.

Sanj lives with his family in Pittsburgh, Pennsylvania.

Made in the USA
Las Vegas, NV
11 May 2022